Who am I?

The Family Tree Explorer

Anthony Adolph

Quercus

For Elvie and Monty Crowe

All that is gold does not glitter,
Not all those who wander are lost;
The old that is strong does not wither,
Deep roots are not reached by the frost.

J.R.R Tolkien

This book belongs to ....

(Grandfather's name)   (Grandmother's name)   (Grandfather's name)   (Grandmother's name)

(Father's name)   (Mother's name)

(My name)

Add your name, your parents and grandparents' names in the
boxes above. Use a pencil, so that you can correct any mistakes.
Once you have filled in the boxes, it will be your family tree.

Contents

Introduction

The more you find out about your ancestors, the better you can answer the question 'who am I?' You will discover more about why you are here, and how you fit into the great wide world around you.

Through exploring your family tree, you may have the opportunity of meeting distant relatives from all over the world, and perhaps be able to visit them in their own countries. You may discover distant connections to artists, writers, warriors and ancient kings, and find out how you are connected to other living creatures into the bargain.

I know this because I have done it myself. It all started when I was about your age. I wanted very much to know more about who I was. My Aunty Ann gave me J.R.R. Tolkien's *The Hobbit* and *The Lord of The Rings*, and I spent hours studying Tolkien's family trees of elves, men and hobbits. I made a similar family tree for a toy bear called Bruno, tracing back six generations to his great, great, great, great grandparents.

My surname is a German one. Like many children growing up in Britain today, I knew from my surname that my family had come here from somewhere else. I asked my parents and grandparents about our family. They said that we had indeed come from Germany to Britain, sometime in the past. That started me wondering. When had my family come here, and why? And where in Germany, exactly, had my ancestors lived?

My journey of discovery had begun. I have found out a lot, but there is so much to find out that I know my journey will go on for all my life.

I have had a wonderful time finding out about myself by exploring my family tree. I do hope you will too. If this book does for you what reading Tolkien did for me, and starts you off on your own fantastic journey of discovery, I shall be very, very pleased indeed.

Anthony Adolph, *Trinovantum*

1

What Granny Remembers: Oral History

Exploring your family tree starts by you asking your parents and grandparents about their own parents and grandparents. It is a simple thing to do, as natural as asking why the world is round, or why robins have red breasts. And it is something we have been doing ever since we were cavemen.

The Origins of Oral History

Long ago, before our ancient ancestors had invented reading or writing, they relied on their memories for everything they knew. They remembered the history of their families. We call this oral history. 'Oral' comes from the Latin *oratio*, meaning 'speech'. So oral history simply means 'spoken history'. In parts of some countries where writing was not introduced until very recently, people can still remember a great deal of oral history.

Oral history exists all over the world. Native Americans remember the names of their ancestors who fought against the European settlers over a hundred years ago. In many African villages, tribesmen can remember the names of ancestors who lived long before the first white people appeared on the savannahs. In Britain, people remember less, because so much has been written down. But oral history still exists – even in your own family.

Your parents and your grandparents will have lots of stories about you and your family.

Your Oral History

By asking questions and listening to the answers, your relatives can become your own personal Internet, chock-full of information about your past. Some will have memories of you as a tiny baby, or perhaps will remember what they were doing the moment they heard you were born.

And that's just the start of it. Weird though it might seem, your parents were once young themselves. Older relatives, if asked, can tell you what your parents were like in their 20s, as teenagers, or even when they were babies themselves.

Most people know who their own parents are, and a lot of people can say the names of their grandparents. Some people might even know the names of family further back still.

The Legend of the Magic Rope

What stories did cavemen tell each other as they sat around their fires in the long winter evenings, thirty thousand years ago, looking out from the mouths of their caves into the inky black night sky? Tales of successful hunts, of strange places they had explored, and myths of how their world was formed, such as how the legendary giant Mammoth made the world's caves by poking her monstrous tusks into the mountainsides. And often, no doubt, they told of the deeds of their ancestors, the members of the family who had died, but whose spirits, everyone believed, still watched over them. And whenever they told such stories, a magical thing would happen.

It might start by one of the children asking a grown-up, 'who am I? Where do I come from?' 'You'll have to ask grandma', would come the reply. Grandma, the oldest living member of the family, would furrow her brow and say 'well, when I was your age, my grandmother used to say…'. And the children would listen to her story.

Grandma's story

As they listened, the children would be looking at grandma's wizened brown face, lined and furrowed like the bark of an old pine tree, and think, 'She could never have been my age!'. And then they would realise, 'but I suppose, once, she must have been!'. Thus would follow their next questions: 'What was your grandma like?'; 'What was her name?'

So grandma would tell the children the names of their ancestors, starting with herself, then the names of her parents, her grandparents, her grandparents' parents, and so on, right back as far as she could remember. And when she had told them all the names, she would make the children repeat them, not once but several times, so they would become fixed in their minds.

In time, the children grew old, and their own grandchildren would ask 'what was your grandma's name?' And they would

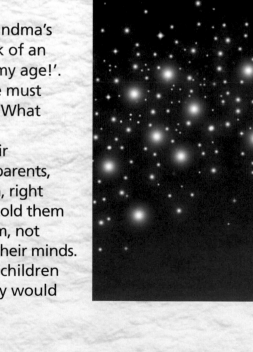

Did you know?

Ask a tohunga

When the English came to New Zealand they wanted to know about the families who already lived there, so they asked a tohunga. Tohungas are specialists who try to remember as many people's ancestors as possible. The Tohunga started telling the English who everybody was, and who their ancestors were, and how they were related. He went on for an hour, and then another hour, and then a day – and he did not stop talking until four days later!

remember the names they had been taught when they were young, and repeat them, so that they could all be learned anew.

Every time this happened, a magical thing also happened. And the magical thing was this: looking out from the mouth of their cave, the inky black night sky made the cave dwellers think that Space and Time were very big and frightening things. Yet when they heard the names of their ancestors being remembered, one after the other, their names seemed to stretch back like a rope of bright stars, right back into the inky blackness of the dim and distant past. And the past stopped being a frightening place, because they had explored it, and knew to whom in their family it had once belonged.

The night sky has always fascinated humanity, particularly when there were no streetlights to make it disappear. Myths and 'personalities' were assigned to stars and patterns of stars in the night sky and these were passed through stoytelling.

Oral History in the Pacific Islands

People all over the world have oral history. Some more good examples come from the islands in the Pacific Ocean. There are thousands of Pacific islands, including Hawaii, Fiji, Samoa, Easter Island and New Zealand. Long before Europeans went there, the Pacific islands were settled gradually by people from south-east Asia, travelling in wooden canoes. A family would settle on one island, and a few generations later some of their descendants would travel on and settle on new islands, spreading ever outwards.

On each island, people can remember long oral histories, stretching back many hundreds of years. The early generations remembered by people on islands that are thousands of miles apart often match up. These must be the names of the ancestors who lived before those particular islands were settled. They have been remembered faithfully for all that time, without anything ever having been written down. On some of the Pacific islands, like Hawaii and New Zealand,

John
(Your name)

Frank
(Your father's name)

William
(Your grandfather's name)

On this map you can see clusters of islands in the Pacific Ocean. The people who live here are descendants of the early settlers from south-east Asia. They have a strong tradition of oral history being passed on from one generation to the next.

old people teach their grandchildren the names of their ancestors in a very special way. They sit on the beach, and each time a wave breaks on the shore they call out the name of an ancestor, and the children repeat it. Wave after wave rolls in and breaks on the sand, and name after name of the ancestors, stretching back into the past, is spoken and remembered. In New Zealand, they call such a list of ancestors' names *Te Here Tangata*, 'the Rope of Mankind'.

They imagine it to be like a rope that stretches right back from you into the distant past, from the dawn of time. The rope does not end with you – it also stretches away into the future too, and includes all the generations who have not yet been born.

Learn your own *Te Here Tangata*

Ask your parents the names of your father's father – your grandfather. Remember what they say. Then ask for the name of his father, your great grandfather. Remember his name as well. See how far back your parents can tell you the names.

Before the New Zealand Maoris knew how to write, they would remember their family tree by imagining it as a rope, stretching back into the past. It was called a *Te Here Tangata*. Why not do the same?

1 Take a thinnish piece of rope (or a thickish piece of string, if that's easier). Tie a series of knots in it, evenly spaced. Imagine that one knot is you, the next is your father, the one after that your grandfather, and so on.

2 When you hold the knot that is you, say your name out loud. Then hold the knot that is your father, and say his name. Then take your grandfather's knot, and say his name.

Charles
(Your great grandfather's name)

Quentin
(Your great great grandfather's name)

3 Look at all those knots, which represent ancestors of yours, whose names you don't know. Don't worry: this book will tell you how to find out who more of them are. Each time you find a new name for an ancestor, you can come back to your *Te Here Tangata* and recite each name starting with you, and add the name of the new ancestor you have discovered.

4 You can do the same thing with your mother's family line as well, and your grandmothers' – as many as you want. To recite your mother's mother's *Te Here Tangata*, start with you (first knot), then your mother (second knot), then her mother (third knot), then her mother, and so on.

2

Writing Down Your Family Story

Our ancestors had extremely good memories, but inevitably a lot of things just ended up being forgotten. Trying not to forget where we come from was a problem for our early ancestors. Luckily for them, along came writing, and things became a lot simpler. Towards the end of this chapter, I will show you how to collect information on your own family, using a Family History Form.

Ancient family histories

However far back a family can remember the oral history of its ancestors, you will reach a point where the names run out. This was one of the problems people hoped to solve by inventing writing. Writing started in Sumeria in the ancient Middle East, in what is now Iraq, about 5,000 years ago. Once writing existed, people no longer had to rely on their memories for everything.

Amongst the very first things that people wrote down were tales of their earliest ancestors. Early writings from around the world tell us who different people thought their ancestors were, and how they had come into being.

Ancient cuneiform writing was made by pressing into soft clay with a stick, and then baking it. This is a letter in cuneiform written well over two thousand years ago.

Family Histories of Kings and Gods: Gilgamesh's Journey

In ancient Babylon, they wrote down the story of a king called Gilgamesh, who lived about 4,700 years ago. Gilgamesh wanted to know where he came from. He set off on a long journey to the edge of the world, where he met a very, very old man called Uta-Napishti. This old man told Gilgamesh that the gods had made humans out of clay, but had then been kept awake by them making too much noise. The gods sent a great flood to destroy noisy mankind, but Uta-Napishti built a boat and survived. According to the story, Uta-Napishti and his wife were therefore the ancestors of Gilgamesh, and of all humans, including us.

Bearded Gilgamesh on his journey across the ancient Middle East to meet his ancestor, Uta-Napishti.

Noah's Flood

When writing spread to Israel, people started writing down the Old Testament, a sacred book for Jews and Muslims, which forms the first part of the Christian Bible. The Old Testament starts with the Book of Genesis, written down about 3,000 years ago. This describes God creating the world, and making the first man and woman, Adam and Eve. Genesis follows the story of Adam and Eve's children, grandchildren and many of their descendants. These included Noah, who is the Jewish equivalent of Uta-Napishti, who built a great boat and survived the Great Flood. Everyone who lived after Noah was believed to be one of his descendants. These include all the main characters in the Bible, including wise King Solomon and even Mary and Joseph, the parents of Jesus. Everyone could be traced back, via Noah, to Adam and Eve.

Hesiod, the First Genealogist

Let us begin our singing from the Muses of Helicon,
That haunt Helicon's great and holy mountain,
And dance on their soft feet round the violet-dark spring
And the altar of the mighty son of Kronos...

These lively lines dance down the centuries from about 2,800 years ago, when writing first spread to Ancient Greece. They are the first lines of a poem called *The Theogony*, written by a poet called Hesiod. While Hesiod was tending his sheep on the slopes of Mount Helicon, he was inspired by the muses or spirits that lived there to write the family history of the gods.

You could say that Hesiod was the very first genealogist, because he is the first person who wrote down a whole family history. He started with the earliest known ancestor, and then told the stories of the ancestor's children, grandchildren, great grandchildren and so on. Hesiod chose the Greek gods as his subject. Sitting quietly on Mount Helicon, Hesiod decided to sort them all out, starting at the beginning.

Hesiod started *The Theogony* with the creation of the world, that emerged from the great Chasm of Chaos. Hesiod then worked down systematically to the offspring of the Chasm – Night, the dark centre of the Earth; and Gaea, the Earth herself. These then had children of their own, including Bright Air and Day, and also Uranos, the God of

This is a very simplified family tree, showing only a tiny part of Hesiod's very complicated genealogy.

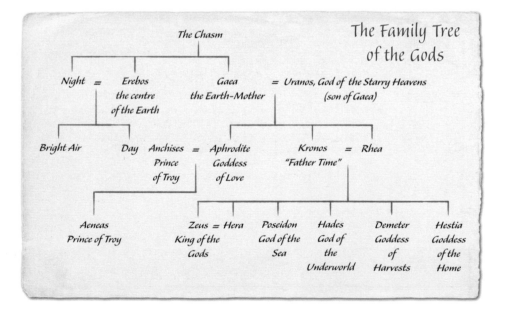

The Family Tree of the Gods

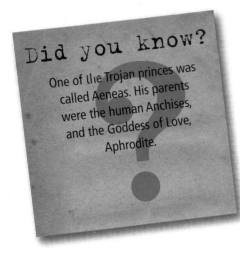
the Starry Heavens. From Gaea and Uranos came the giant Titans, including Kronos and Rhea. Kronos rebelled against his father Uranos and murdered him by chopping off part of his body. This part of Uranos fell into the foaming sea, and out of the water came Aphrodite, the Goddess of Love. Kronos himself was the father of the mighty Zeus, King of the Gods, who was father of many more gods in turn.

Since Hesiod's time, many people have been inspired to explore and write similar histories of families of gods, kings, and ordinary people.

A Goddess in the Family

Homer, a poet who lived about the same time as Hesiod, wrote a poem called *The Iliad*. It tells of an ancient war fought between gods and men over a beautiful city called Troy, which was besieged and eventually destroyed.

In *The Iliad*, Homer also described how many of the heroes who fought at Troy had gods and goddesses for fathers or mothers. Later, many Greek kings claimed to be descended from the heroes of *The Iliad*, so in many cases they actually thought they had gods for ancestors too.

One of the Trojan princes was called Aeneas. His parents were the human Anchises, and the Goddess of Love, Aphrodite. The story of how Aeneas fled from the ruins of Troy to Italy, and founded Rome, was told in a famous Roman poem, *The Aeneid,* by Virgil. The famous Roman emperor Julius Caesar, who lived just over 2,000 years ago, believed that Aeneas – and therefore Aeneas's mother Aphrodite – were his distant ancestors.

No wonder Julius Caesar was so fearless in battle, for he genuinely believed he had a goddess for his ancestor.

The painting on the opposite page shows brave Aeneas carrying his father Anchises from the burning ruins of the ancient city of Troy. It was painted by Charles-André van Loo in 1729 and is in the Louvre Museum, Paris.

The Kings of Britain

Virgil's *Aeneid* was such a fantastic story that it inspired many other writers. About 900 years ago, a Welsh writer, Geoffrey of Monmouth, wrote *The History of the Kings of Britain*. This family history starts with Brutus, a great grandson of Aeneas. While out hunting, Brutus fired an arrow that accidentally killed his father. Brutus was sent into exile, and sailed away with his followers to Spain, and then to Britain. He landed at Totnes in Devon, and killed the giants who lived there. Brutus founded a city in south-east England, which he called Trinovantum or New Troy, and which is now called London. Geoffrey then tells the story of Brutus's descendants, the legendary kings of Britain, including King Arthur.

The stories of Gilgamesh, Zeus, Aeneas and Brutus are examples of early family histories of kings and gods. How true they are, I cannot say – some people believe them, and others don't.

Most people nowadays do not believe they are descended from gods. But there are plenty of family trees that go back from the present day to people who certainly believed that they were.

You can see statues of the giants whom Brutus fought, in London's Guildhall: the giant below is called Magog.

The Brutus Stone, shown right, in Totnes is said to be the stone on which Brutus first stepped when he came ashore.

Dynasties of the Sun and the Moon

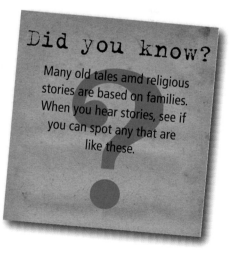

In Indian mythology, all ancient kings claimed to be descendents of either the Sun God or the Moon God.

Imagine being able to trace your family tree right back to the Sun and the Moon!

Family trees are an important part of Hinduism, one of the main religions of India. All Hindu families who belong to the Kshatriya (kash-art-ri-a) or Warrior Caste claim descent, one way or another, from the ancient kings of India, who ruled more than 3,000 years ago. The pedigrees of these ancient kings are recorded in sacred books, called Puranas. These trace the kings back to nothing less than the Sun and the Moon themselves.

It is said that Vivaswan, the Sun God, had a son called Manu Vivasvata, who was the first human. Manu had nine sons and a daughter called Ila, who married a son of the Moon – and they had human children too. The descendants of Manu's sons are the Solar (Sun) Dynasty, and the descendants of Ila are the Lunar (Moon) Dynasty. Many famous figures in Hindu mythology belong to these dynasties, as do millions of Hindu kshatriyas in India and Britain today.

Did you know?

Many old tales amd religious stories are based on families. When you hear stories, see if you can spot any that are like these.

Recording your family history

1 Copy this Family History Form.

2 Ask one of your parents the questions, and write down the answers on a copy of the form. Some questions will not apply to the person you are asking, such as 'date of death'. Just cross these out.

3 Ask the same questions of your other parent, then of your grandparents, and then of any other relatives you can. You will be able to ask some people face-to-face now. You may be due to see other relatives soon, perhaps at birthdays, weddings or religious festivals like Christmas or Diwali.

4 If you know you are going somewhere where you will see relatives, take some Family History Forms with you. You can also increase your collection of filled-in Family History Forms by contacting relatives by telephone, letter or e-mail.

5 Once you have asked everyone you can who is alive, start asking your parents and grandparents about relatives who have died. For example, if your grandfather's parents have died, you can ask him to help you fill in a form for each of his parents. He may also be able to give you some answers about his grandparents, and maybe even earlier ancestors.

6 The question about 'interesting stories' is there because it might lead to you being told all sorts of unexpected things about your family history. It is like a lucky dip at a fairground: you ask the question, and wait and see what stories you will be told. If you run out of space, carry on writing down what you are told on other sheets of paper, stapling them to the form when you have finished.

TIP It is always worth asking relatives if they know how to contact other, more distant cousins. Your aunt may be in touch with a cousin, for example, so you can find out how the cousin in related to you. You can then contact that cousin and ask them about themselves. They may in turn be in touch with another even more distant cousin of yours, of whom you've never heard, and who might live on the other side of the world – but who might be perfectly happy to answer your questions by e-mail.

Congratulations, by the way: you have just become a genealogist.

FAMILY HISTORY FORM:

This form was filled in by .... on [date] -- ---- 2-----

Relative's full name (including any middle names):

Their date of birth:

Their place of birth:

Their father's name:

Their mother's name:

Names of brothers and sisters:

This person's jobs and occupations:

Their religion:

Name of partner(s):

Date and place of wedding(s):   date

Names and dates of birth of children:

Date of death:

Place of death:

Where buried or cremated:

Interesting stories:

continue on extra paper

Now, you can use the information on your Family History Forms to make a family tree.

3

Making Your Family Tree

Lists of names and relationships can become very complicated. Family trees are a really good way of showing how all the names on your Family History Forms fit together. They can make all the names and dates a lot less confusing. In fact, family trees have a long history themselves.

Drawing family trees

It's best to do this in pencil, using a large piece of paper.
A good thing about family trees is that they often grow
too big for one piece of paper. If this happens to you, you
can sticky-tape on new pieces of paper. It's best to put the
tape on the back, so that it does not stop you writing across
the joins.

Drawing your Family tree

Key

=	indicates a couple
b.	born
bpt or **c**.	baptised or christened (same thing)
d.	died
bur.	buried
d.s.p.	died without having had children
m.	married

Step 1

A) Write your own name in the middle of the piece of paper, at the bottom.

B) Next to you, write your brothers and sisters, if you have any. Put them in order of age, oldest on the left, youngest on the right.

C) Under the names, write the dates of birth and places of birth. Use the abbreviation 'b.' for 'born'. You don't have to, but it's a good idea to write the surnames in capitals, so that other people will not misread them.

D) Connect you and your brothers and sisters up by drawing a line across the top of the names, with short lines coming down to each name.

TIP

If a couple had an official marriage or civil partnership, add the date. If the couple is simply lived together, use the '=' sign but do not include a date

Step 2

Now it is time for the generation before you. For this, you can refer to the Family History Forms you filled in when you started asking your parents questions.

A) Above your name, write the names of your father and mother. Keep your father on the left, and your mother on the right.

B) Between them, draw an equals sign (=) that shows they produced children together. Draw a line down from the equals sign to connect to the line linking the children (if they only had one child, you, then draw the line coming directly down to you).

C) Under their names, add their dates and places of birth.

D) You can also add their jobs.

E) If your parents are married, then add the date and place of marriage, starting with 'm.' for 'married'.

First diagram

Edgar Arthur SMITH
b. 2 Sept. 1937, Luton
d. 14 Feb. 1999, Luton
Chemist

= **Nellie Agnes CRUMP**
b. 8 Aug. 1938, Bedford
m. 12 Oct 1962, Luton

Percival GRAY
b. 1 Jan. 1945
Nottingham
Dentist

= **Gladys Doris MUIR**
b. 2 April 1943, London
m. 17 July 1970, Oxford
d. 8 Aug. 2006, Weybridge

James Edward SMITH
b. 2 April 1963, Luton
Chemist

William David SMITH
b. 9 Sept. 1968, Luton
Office manager

= **Emma Lucy GRAY**
b. 10 Oct. 1973, Oxford
m. 18 March 1994, Oxford
Doctor

Mary GRAY
b. 6 April 1971, Oxford
m. 10 April 1996, Oxford
= Nathan OATES

D

Anne Marie SMITH
b. 2 Feb. 1995
Guildford

A **John William SMITH**
C b. 7 Aug. 1997
Guildford

B **Henry James SMITH**
b. 12 Dec. 1999
Weybridge

Harry OATES
b. 4 Feb. 2000
Newcastle

b. born

Second diagram

Edgar Arthur SMITH
b. 2 Sept. 1937, Luton
d. 14 Feb. 1999, Luton
Chemist

= **Nellie Agnes CRUMP**
b. 8 Aug. 1938, Bedford
m. 12 Oct 1962, Luton

Percival GRAY
b. 1 Jan. 1945
Nottingham
Dentist

= **Gladys Doris MUIR**
b. 2 April 1943, London
m. 17 July 1970, Oxford
d. 8 Aug. 2006, Weybridge

d. died

= indicates a couple

James Edward SMITH
b. 2 April 1963, Luton
Chemist

A **William David SMITH**
C b. 9 Sept. 1968, Luton
D Office manager

B = **Emma Lucy GRAY**
b. 10 Oct. 1973, Oxford
E m. 18 March 1994, Oxford
Doctor

Mary GRAY
b. 6 April 1971, Oxford
m. 10 April 1996, Oxford
= Nathan OATES

Anne Marie SMITH
b. 2 Feb. 1995
Guildford

John William SMITH
b. 7 Aug. 1997
Guildford

m. married

Henry James SMITH
b. 12 Dec. 1999
Weybridge

Harry OATES
b. 4 Feb. 2000
Newcastle

Step 3

Now it is time to add your parents' brothers and sisters – this is where you may have to start sticky-taping on new pieces of paper.

A) Put them in order of age, except for your parents, who you may have to put out of order – your father will have to appear on the right of his brothers and sisters, and your mother will have to appear to the left of hers.

B) If any of your uncles and aunts have married, you can add their partners' names, either next to them, or underneath them, as space permits, with an equals sign and the date of their marriage.

C) If they have children, draw a line down from the parents and add the names and dates of birth of your cousins.

Step 4

Time for the third generation, your grandparents.

A) Again, you can use the notes you made on your Family History Forms to check their correct names, dates of birth and marriage, occupations and, if they have died, their dates and places of death.

B) You can connect them to their children as before, with lines coming down from the equals signs between them.

Step 5

A) Then keep going, adding your grandparents' brothers and sisters; their children and grandchildren (who would be your second cousins); your grandparents' parents (your great grandparents), their brothers and sisters and descendants; and so on.

B) As you find out more about your family, you will be able to add extra details. And yes, you will need lots of extra pieces of paper, and a great deal of sticky-tape.

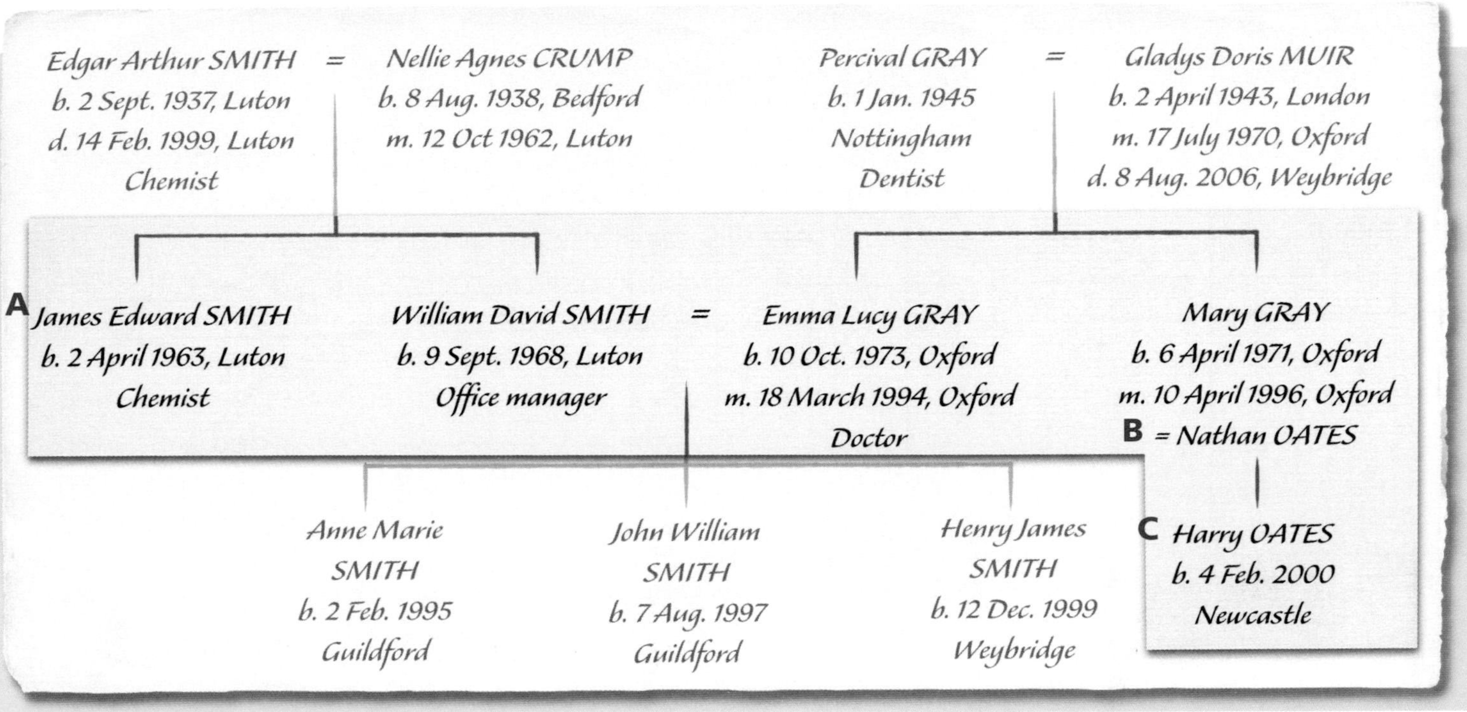

Diagram 1

A Edgar Arthur SMITH
b. 2 Sept. 1937, Luton
d. 14 Feb. 1999, Luton
Chemist

=

Nellie Agnes CRUMP
b. 8 Aug. 1938, Bedford
m. 12 Oct 1962, Luton

Percival GRAY
b. 1 Jan. 1945
Nottingham
Dentist

=

Gladys Doris MUIR
b. 2 April 1943, London
m. 17 July 1970, Oxford
d. 8 Aug. 2006, Weybridge

James Edward SMITH
b. 2 April 1963, Luton
Chemist

William David SMITH
b. 9 Sept. 1968, Luton
Office manager

=

Emma Lucy GRAY
b. 10 Oct. 1973, Oxford
m. 18 March 1994, Oxford
Doctor

Mary GRAY
b. 6 April 1971, Oxford
m. 10 April 1996, Oxford
B = Nathan OATES

Anne Marie
SMITH
b. 2 Feb. 1995
Guildford

John William
SMITH
b. 7 Aug. 1997
Guildford

Henry James
SMITH
b. 12 Dec. 1999
Weybridge

C Harry OATES
b. 4 Feb. 2000
Newcastle

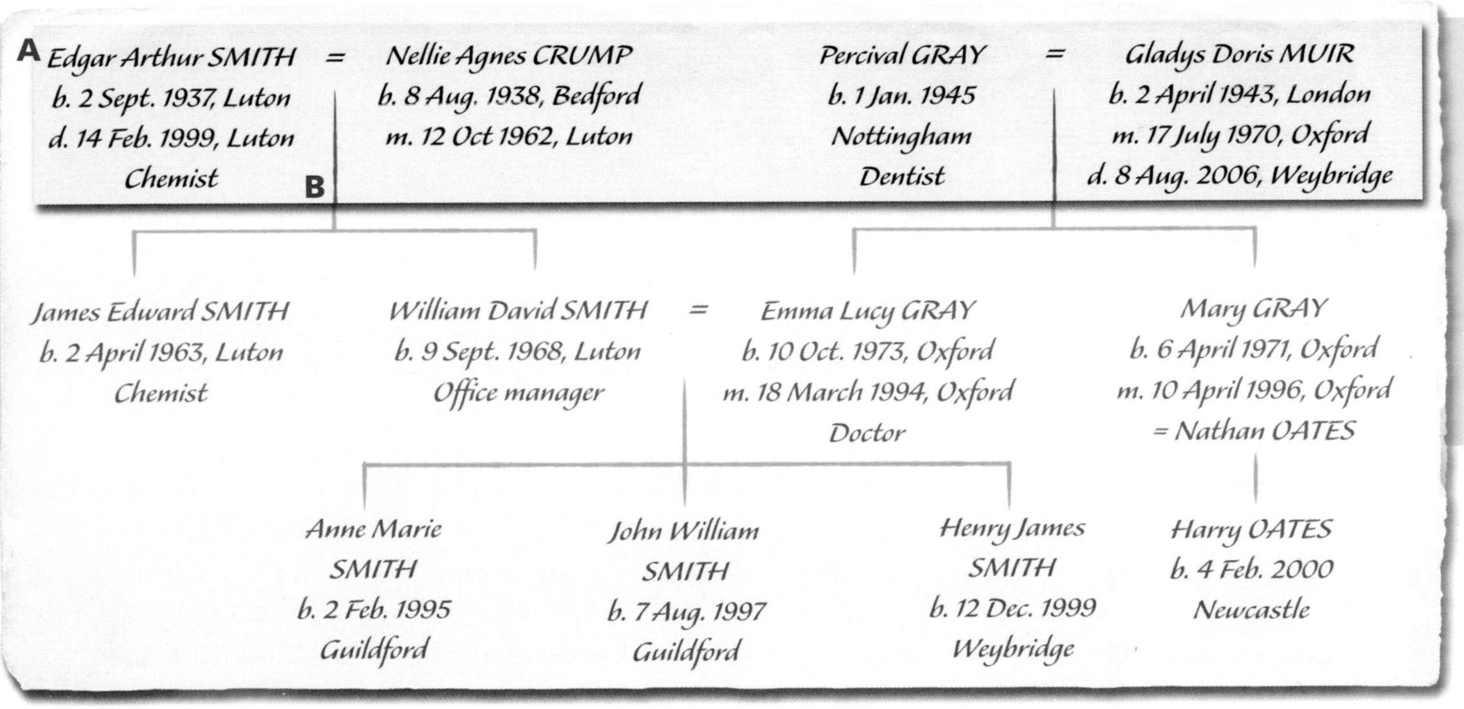

Diagram 2

A Edgar Arthur SMITH
b. 2 Sept. 1937, Luton
d. 14 Feb. 1999, Luton
Chemist

=

Nellie Agnes CRUMP
b. 8 Aug. 1938, Bedford
m. 12 Oct 1962, Luton

B

Percival GRAY
b. 1 Jan. 1945
Nottingham
Dentist

=

Gladys Doris MUIR
b. 2 April 1943, London
m. 17 July 1970, Oxford
d. 8 Aug. 2006, Weybridge

James Edward SMITH
b. 2 April 1963, Luton
Chemist

William David SMITH
b. 9 Sept. 1968, Luton
Office manager

=

Emma Lucy GRAY
b. 10 Oct. 1973, Oxford
m. 18 March 1994, Oxford
Doctor

Mary GRAY
b. 6 April 1971, Oxford
m. 10 April 1996, Oxford
= Nathan OATES

Anne Marie
SMITH
b. 2 Feb. 1995
Guildford

John William
SMITH
b. 7 Aug. 1997
Guildford

Henry James
SMITH
b. 12 Dec. 1999
Weybridge

Harry OATES
b. 4 Feb. 2000
Newcastle

Complicated family trees

Family trees can be hard to draw, because families produce random numbers of children. One couple may have one child, which is very easy to draw, but another may produce ten. If all ten children have big families, then the family tree on that side becomes enormous. Another problem comes when two members of one family marry two members of another – two brothers marrying two sisters, for example. It can take some time working out how best to show this on a family tree, and is usually involves having one line looping over another, like the one below.

These complications exist in real families. You just have to show them as best you can on the family tree. But the more complicated your family tree, the more interesting it becomes.

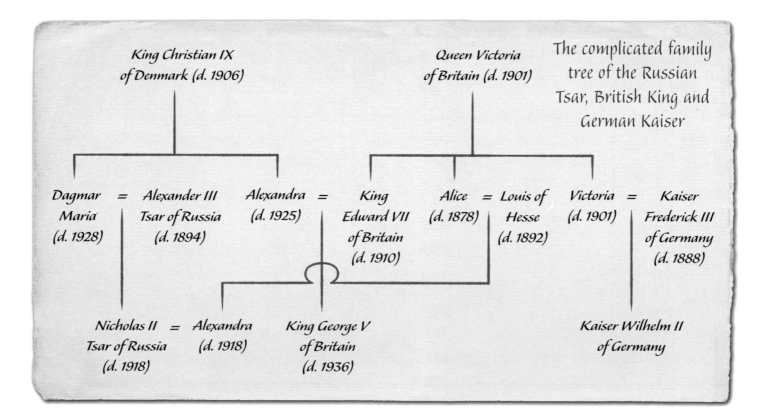

The complicated family tree of the Russian Tsar, British King and German Kaiser

King Christian IX of Denmark (d. 1906)

Queen Victoria of Britain (d. 1901)

Dagmar Maria (d. 1928) = Alexander III Tsar of Russia (d. 1894)

Alexandra (d. 1925) = King Edward VII of Britain (d. 1910)

Alice (d. 1878) = Louis of Hesse (d. 1892)

Victoria (d. 1901) = Kaiser Frederick III of Germany (d. 1888)

Nicholas II Tsar of Russia (d. 1918) = Alexandra (d. 1918)

King George V of Britain (d. 1936)

Kaiser Wilhelm II of Germany

Versions of family trees

You may end up redrawing your family tree several times. Do not worry. I've been tracing mine for over 25 years, and have drawn dozens of versions of it. Part of the fun is redrawing family trees to show new things you have found out.

As you learn more about your family, you might want to draw separate family trees for each grandparent. Following the example on page 27, you could draw an individual family tree for the Smiths like this:

Following the example on page 27,

TIP

Instead of showing the ancestors of the people who married into the family, you can summarise them (by writing 'daughter of Percival and Gladys Doris Gray' under Emma Lucy's name, for example). As you can see, this gives you more room to add on other branches of the Smith family.

An individual family tree for the Smith family

Edgar Arthur SMITH = Nellie Agnes CRUMP
b. 2 Sept. 1937, Luton   b. 8 Aug. 1938, Bedford
d. 14 Feb. 1999, Luton   m. 12 Oct. 1962, Luton
Chemist

James Edward SMITH   William David SMITH = Emma Lucy
b. 2 April 1963, Luton   b. 9 Sept. 1968, Luton   daughter of Percival
Chemist   Office manager   and Gladys Doris GRAY
                                                      b. 10 Oct. 1973, Oxford
                                                      m. 18 March 1994, Oxford
                                                      Doctor

Anne Marie   John William   Henry James
SMITH   SMITH   SMITH
b. 2 Feb. 1995   b. 7 Aug. 1997   b. 12 Dec. 1999
Guildford   Guildford   Weybridge

Simplified family trees

Another type of family tree just shows your direct ancestors. After you have done a lot of research, you will have mounds of notes, and big, complicated family trees for different parts of your family.

You will probably be confused as to how they all fit together, so it's very satisfying to draw a simple chart just showing the names and, if there is room, years of birth and death of your direct ancestors, your grandparents, grandparents and so on.

You can leave out almost all details, because the aim is just to produce a picture of what you know of your ancestry overall.

As you work up the page and space grows limited, include less detail, and you can even write the names on their sides to save more space.

By doing this, you will be able to see who all your known ancestors were. You will also see the gaps where you have not yet found out who is who.

TIP

If you can't, at first, find all the names in your family history remember to leave space for them by using question marks. This means you will be able to fit them in later, when you have found them.

William SMITH = Catherine GRAY
Frederick STEWART = Eliza McNEE
Thomas EVANS = Eliza HOLBROOK
Jeffrey ARCHER = Catherine EMERSON

Albert SMITH = Eliza STEWART
John EVANS = Annie ARCHER

Arthur SMITH = Annie EVANS
b. 1910   b. 1908
d. 1970   d. 1958

Edgar SMITH =
b. 1937
d. 1999

On this chart the space has been used more effectively, by writing the names on their sides. This means that you don't need such a large piece of paper.

A simplified Smith and Gray family tree

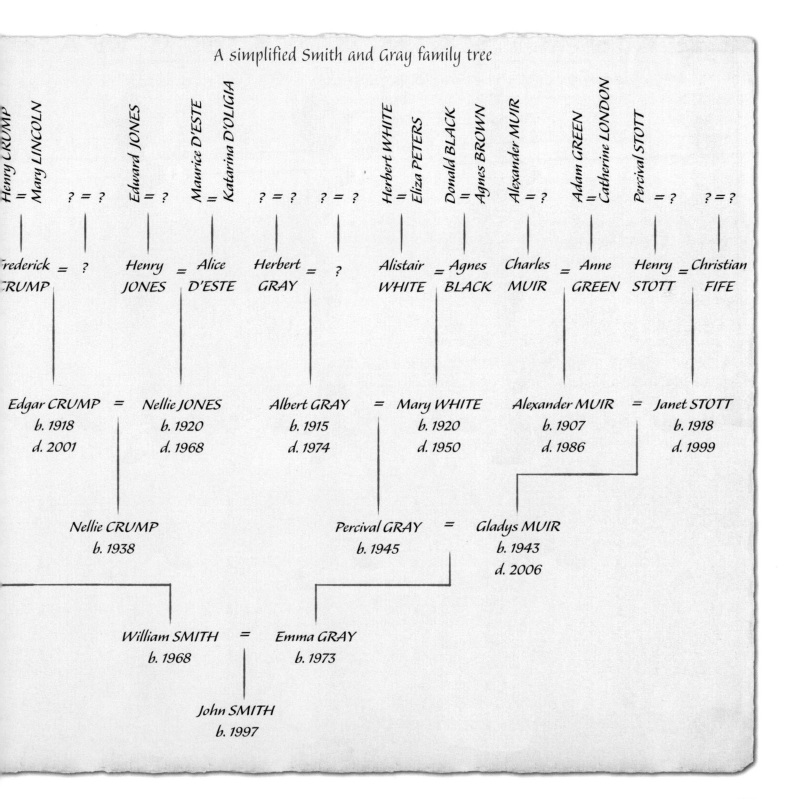

Henry CRUMP = Mary LINCOLN

? = ?

Edward JONES = ?

Maurice D'ESTE = Katarina D'OLIGIA

? = ?

? = ?

Herbert WHITE = Eliza PETERS

Donald BLACK = Agnes BROWN

Alexander MUIR = ?

Adam GREEN = Catherine LONDON

Percival STOTT = ?

? = ?

Frederick CRUMP = ?

Henry JONES = Alice D'ESTE

Herbert GRAY = ?

Alistair WHITE = Agnes BLACK

Charles MUIR = Anne GREEN

Henry STOTT = Christian FIFE

Edgar CRUMP
b. 1918
d. 2001
= Nellie JONES
b. 1920
d. 1968

Albert GRAY
b. 1915
d. 1974
= Mary WHITE
b. 1920
d. 1950

Alexander MUIR
b. 1907
d. 1986
= Janet STOTT
b. 1918
d. 1999

Nellie CRUMP
b. 1938

Percival GRAY
b. 1945
= Gladys MUIR
b. 1943
d. 2006

William SMITH
b. 1968
= Emma GRAY
b. 1973

John SMITH
b. 1997

The History of Family Trees

If you visited a big Roman house about two thousand years ago, you would go through the front door into a wide entrance hall. Here you might very well have seen a collection of wax face masks, called *imagines* ('im-a-geens', similar to our word 'image', meaning 'picture'). Each *imagine* was modelled to resemble the face of an ancestor. Under each mask, the family wrote the ancestor's name. They would then string ribbons between the masks (or draw them), to show how the ancestors were connected to each other.

The whole display was called a *stemma*. On holidays and festivals Romans would place laurel wreaths on the masks to show that the ancestors were still remembered with respect. It was also a good way of showing off your grand ancestors, if you had any. Visitors to Julius Caesar's house would have seen his *stemma*, showing how he was descended from the goddess Aphrodite. They would have been very impressed, and that was the whole point.

This painted plaster mask from the Roman city of Hermopolis, Egypt, is very like the *imagines* that Romans displayed in their homes.

Old family trees

About a thousand years ago, in the Middle Ages, people thought of drawing charts, rather like these *stemma*, but on paper. Instead of a wax mask, they drew a circle and wrote the person's name in it. Instead of ribbons to connect each person, they drew lines. They would draw lines fanning out from parents to each of their children, and more lines fanning out from the children to their children in turn. An example is on p.39.

All these radiating lines made the charts look like drawings of upside down trees – so they started calling them family trees. Today, we still talk about families having different 'branches', just as if they really were trees.

The picture on the facing page shows a made-up modern Smith family tree, drawn in the syle of an ancient Roman *stemma*. The word 'Gens' in the title was Latin for family.

STEMMA OF
GENS SMITHUS

ALFREDUS.SMITHUS

CATHERINA.SMITHA

FRANKUS.SMITHUS

JOANA.SMITHA

EDWARDUS.SMITHUS

ELIZABETHA.SMITHA

JOSEPHUS.SMITHUS

HENRICUS.SMITHUS

JOHNUS.SMITHUS

MARIA.SMITHA

Pedigrees

There's another old word for family trees – pedigrees. The way this term came about sounds really odd, but it's true. In the trees like the one on p39, the circle (containing the parent) with lines fanning out to other circles (the children) was thought to look a bit like a bird's footprint. In particular, it looked like the footprint of a crane (which is like a heron or stork), that was often seen in the soft mud on the banks of rivers. The old French for 'Crane's foot' is *pied de gru*. If you say 'pied de gru' very quickly a few times you can see that it really does sound like the word 'pedigree', and that's how the word came about.

Nowadays, the words 'family tree' and 'pedigree' mean the same thing – a chart showing how all the members of the family are related to each other.

In the background of this page you can see the footprints of the crane, which inspired the term *pied de gru*, French for 'crane's foot'.

Genealogy

A further word whose meaning you might want to know is 'genealogy'. Genealogy is the name we give the whole art of discovering ancestors and drawing family trees. It comes from two Greek words (the ancient Greeks were absolutely potty about ancestors) – γενεα (pronounced 'genea' and meaning 'family'), and λόγος (pronounced 'logos', meaning 'knowledge'). The word therefore means 'knowledge about families', which is a pretty fair description of what genealogy is.

In ancient Greek households there were sometimes sculptures of families, like this one. The family are shown on the left – father, mother, grown up son and daughter, and two small children. They are shown praying to Asclepios, the God of Medicine, and his own family, to be granted good health.

Using your imagination

There are many ways of drawing family trees, and there are no rules: you can include as much or as little information as you want. You can draw your family tree any way you so desire – as a tree, or a flower, or a series of planets, or whatever your imagination suggests.

Try constructing your family tree using this stunning method of concentric circles radiating out from the centre with you at the middle.

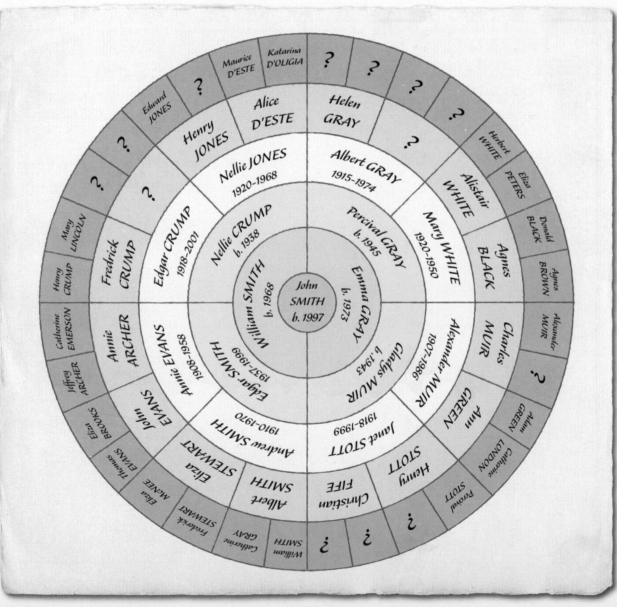

Creating your family tree as a Roman *stemma*

To create a Roman *stemma*, you will need a board, some plasticine, some paper labels, glue, and ribbon (you can use string, but bright ribbon will look grander).

1 Take some modelling clay and make a small *imagine* or mask of your own face. A mask is shaped like a face – like half a ball, slightly flattened. Make it about the size of a golf ball.

2 You can model the nose, ears and eyebrows, and make the mouth and eyes by cutting holes, if you like.

3 Put your mask in the middle of the board, at the bottom.

4 Glue a label underneath saying your name. Write the name in Roman style, using bold capital letters, and put a dot between each word, the way the Romans did. Men tended to have '-us' on the end of their names, and women '-a', so John Smith could be written 'JOHNUS.SMITHUS' and Catherine Smith 'CATHERINA.SMITHA', to make them sound more Roman.

5 Make masks of both your parents. Put one to your right and the other to your left, and glue labels underneath.

6 Tie a bow in a piece of ribbon and glue it between your two parents. This shows that they are a couple. Then take a piece of ribbon and glue one end to the edge of your mask, and the other to the bow, to connect you to your parents.

7 Make masks showing your grandparents' faces. Put your father's parents above his mask, and your mother's parents above her mask. Add the labels saying who they are, and connect your parents to their parents using other pieces of ribbon. You can then add any grandparents and earlier ancestors you know about in the same way, arranging the masks as best you can on the piece of board.

TIP

Books and websites about the Romans will show you how they decorated their houses, and will give you ideas for filling in blank spaces. They liked pictures of bunches of grapes, fish and birds, and borders or edges made of repeated patterns.

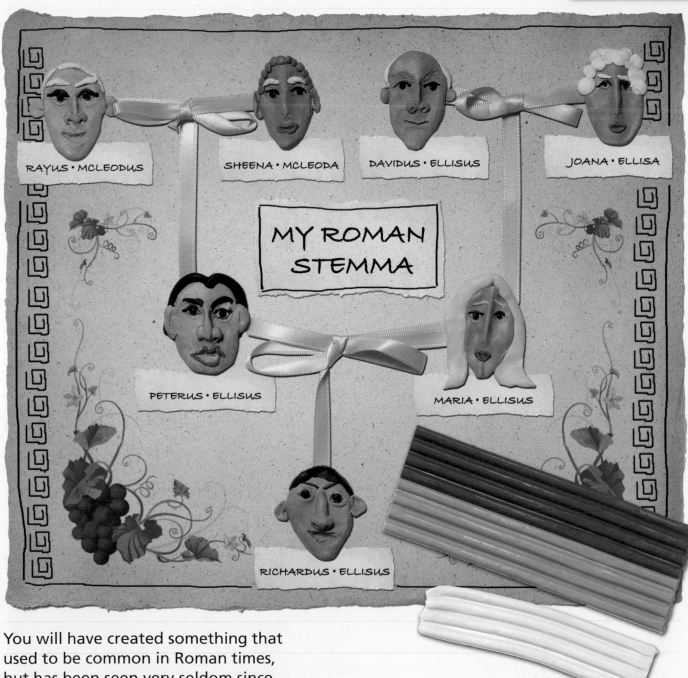

RAYUS • MCLEODUS

SHEENA • MCLEODA

DAVIDUS • ELLISUS

JOANA • ELLISA

MY ROMAN STEMMA

PETERUS • ELLISUS

MARIA • ELLISUS

RICHARDUS • ELLISUS

You will have created something that used to be common in Roman times, but has been seen very seldom since. But what a good way to remember who your ancestors are!

Creating your family tree as a *pied de gru* or pedigree.

You will need a large piece of paper, an egg cup, a ruler and as many coloured pens as you possess.

1 At the bottom of the paper, draw a circle round the egg cup. Write your name in it: you can make your writing look old-fashioned by using 'Gothic' script, adding extra loops, and turning the curves of letters into sharp angles.

2 Above your name, use the egg cups to draw two circles next to each other, and fill in your parents' names. Don't connect them using an equals sign, because this was not done in the Middle Ages, but instead draw the circles so that they touch.

3 Draw a straight line coming down from your parents, starting where their circles touch, and ending with you.

4 Above your parents, draw four more circles and fill in your grandparents' names, connecting them to your parents with straight lines.

5 If you want to add any brothers and sisters, give them circles as well, and connect them to their parents using straight lines.

6 Illustrate your pedigree with pictures of where ancestors lived, or objects to do with their work, or family pets or favourite animals, as in the illustration opposite. If your ancestors were soldiers, you could draw their weapons, or if they loved gardening you could draw some of the plants they grew.

7 Roll your *pied de gru* up to make a scroll, and tie a ribbon round it: this is how people in Medieval times kept their written records.

TIP

Medieval pedigrees were often of grand families, who usually had coats of arms. These were often included. If your family does not have a coat of arms, make one up. You can read about coats of arms in chapter twelve.

In the picture on the facing page you can see how in Medieval times, drawers of *pied de gru* might have filled blank spaces with pictures. Here the heads and shoulders of the people in the pedigrees are drawn straight above the circles. You can draw your favourite pets, or even little scenes, for instance a church where a couple in the pedigree were married.

4

Grandpa's Sister's Daughter: Who's Who in Your Family?

The more you think about it, the more you realise that there are a lot of people out there who are related to you. There are grandparents, cousins, step-brothers and step-sisters – it can all become very confusing!

The Story of Dracula

Dracula is a book written by Victorian writer Bram Stoker, which was later made into many horror films. It is about a Count of Transylvania (in modern Romania) who becomes a vampire, and lives by sucking human blood. It is said that the worst thing about having your blood sucked by a vampire is that you become one yourself.

Thank goodness, vampires don't exist in real life. But there was a real Count Dracula. His full name was Vlad III Dracula, Prince of Valachia which, like Transylvania, is part of modern Romania, in south-east Europe. Nicknamed 'Vlad the Impaler', he had his enemies impaled, or skewered on the end of sharp sticks, and took an evil enjoyment in watching them die horrible deaths. Not only was this evil Vlad Dracula a real person, but he also appears in the family tree of His Royal Highness Prince William.

Vlad III of Valachia, known as Vlad the Impaler, died in 1462. This portrait was painted around 100 years after he died.

Dracula: Prince William's ancestral uncle?

Prince William is the grandson of Queen Elizabeth II. Queen Elizabeth's own grandmother, Queen Mary, was a German princess. She was born in a place called Teck in southern Germany. Her own grandmother was called Countess Claudine Rhédey de Kis-Rhéde (which is pronounced 'ready to kiss: ready'). Countess Claudine's family were from Hungary, which is further east. Over the centuries, the countess's family had intermarried with families from Transylvania, which is a bit further east still, and her ancestors included Vlad IV (the fourth) of Valachia. Vlad IV was the brother of the evil Vlad III 'Count Dracula' (yes, both brothers were called Vlad. It must have been very confusing when they were growing up, but they were quite an odd family anyway).

'Dracula' was therefore the brother of an ancestor of Prince William's. So that makes 'Dracula' the ancestral uncle of Prince William. In your family tree, you might find an interesting character who was the brother or sister of one of your ancestors. You can say that they were your ancestral uncle or ancestral aunt. But I doubt many of you will find an ancestral uncle who was a vampire!

How people are related

We human beings are very interested in how we are related to each other. We have lots of different words to describe different sorts of relationship. These are the main ones:

Parents These are your mother and father.

Aunts and uncles Aunts are women who are sisters of either your mother or father. Uncles are men who are brothers of either your mother or father. We use the same terms for husbands and wives of uncles and aunts. If your aunt Mary marries James, then James becomes your uncle, even though he is not a blood relation, and you become James's niece or nephew.

Nieces and nephews
These are the children of your brothers and sisters. You are the niece or nephew of your parents' brothers and sisters, your uncles and aunts.

First cousins These are the children of your uncles and aunts. That means that you and your first cousins share one set of grandparents.

Grandparents These are the parents of your own parents. You can tell them apart by calling your mother's parents your maternal grandparents, and your father's parents your paternal grandparents (*mater* and *pater* are the Latin for 'mother' and 'father').

Great aunts and great uncles These are the brothers and sisters of your grandparents.

Second cousins These are the grandchildren of your great aunts and uncles. Put another way, they are the children of your parents' first cousins.

Third cousins These are the great grandchildren of your great great aunts and uncles.

Great grandparents
These are the parents of your grandparents, or, put another way, the grand-parents of your parents. On the family tree, they appear three lines above you. You are a great grandchild of your great grandparents.

Great great aunts and uncles These are the brothers and sisters of your great grandparents. Each generation back you go, you simply add another 'great'.

Great great great grandparents These are the grandparents of your grandparents. For each generation you go back up the family tree, you just add an extra 'great'. Your grandparent's grandparent's grandparent's grandparent is your great great great great great great grandparent. There are six 'greats' there, so you can also write '6 x great grandparents'.

Other common terms

Ancestors This term is used for anyone from whom you are directly descended - your great grandparents, grandparents and even your parents are your ancestors. Some people use the term for anyone in their family tree, including ancestral uncles and aunts (see below) and cousins. However these are not ancestors, because you are not directly descended from them.

Forebears or forefathers These are other words for 'ancestors'. You can talk about your great great (etc) grandparents as your ancestors, forebears or forefathers, though obviously 'forefathers' only applies to men.

Descendants This is the opposite of ancestors. Descendants are the children, grandchildren, or great (etc) grandchildren of ancestors.

Ancestral uncles and ancestral aunts This is an easier way of describing a great great great (etc) aunt or uncle, in other words, the brother or sister or an ancestor, however remote.

Brothers- and sisters-in-law These are people who have married into the family. If Brian marries your sister Jane, then Brian becomes your brother-in-law.

Cousins once and twice removed This can become marvellously complicated. It's best to draw a family tree showing how you and your cousin are descended from the same grandparent, great grandparent (or whatever), but keeping each generation on the same line. If you and your cousin appear on the same level, then you are direct first, second or more cousins.

If you appear on different levels, then you are cousins so many times removed. If the difference is of one generation, then you are cousins once removed. If the difference is two generations, then you are cousins twice removed. It gets even more confusing now, because the degree of cousinship depends on whose point of view you take.

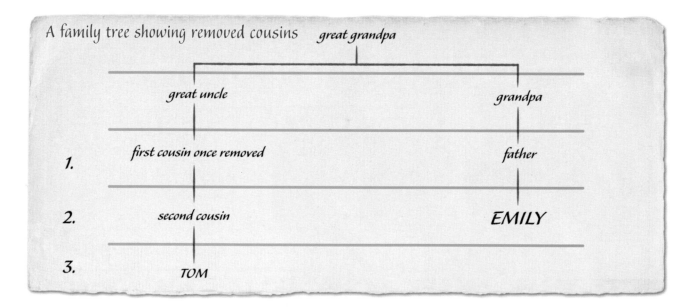

A family tree showing removed cousins

In the diagram above, all the relationships are described from Emily's point of view. Tom is the son of her second cousin, he is her second cousin once removed. However, things are different from Tom's point of view: looking across the family tree, he is on the level where Emily's children would be, if she had any. Those children would be his third cousins. Emily is a generation removed from them; so Emily is Tom's third cousin once removed.

Foster parents, foster brothers and foster sisters If you are looked after by other people, those people are called your foster parents. If those parents have other children of their own, or have fostered other children, those children are your foster brothers and foster sisters.

Adopted parents, adopted brothers and adopted sisters If you are adopted by parents who did not give birth to you, then those parents are called your adopted parents. If those parents have other children of their own, or have adopted other children, those children are your adopted brothers and adopted sisters.

Adopted children can refer to their original parents, brothers and sisters as 'birth' parents (etc). The terms 'natural' and 'biological' are used sometimes, too.

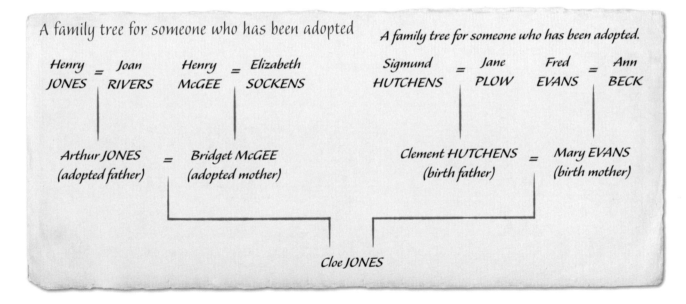

A family tree for someone who has been adopted.

The diagram above shows how fostering and adopting can give people two families – the original one, from their birth parents, and the new adopted or foster family. You have two sets of parents, two sets of brothers and sisters, two sets of four grandparents, and so on. Here's how you can draw a double family tree, if you would like to show both (though you may need an enormous sheet of paper!).

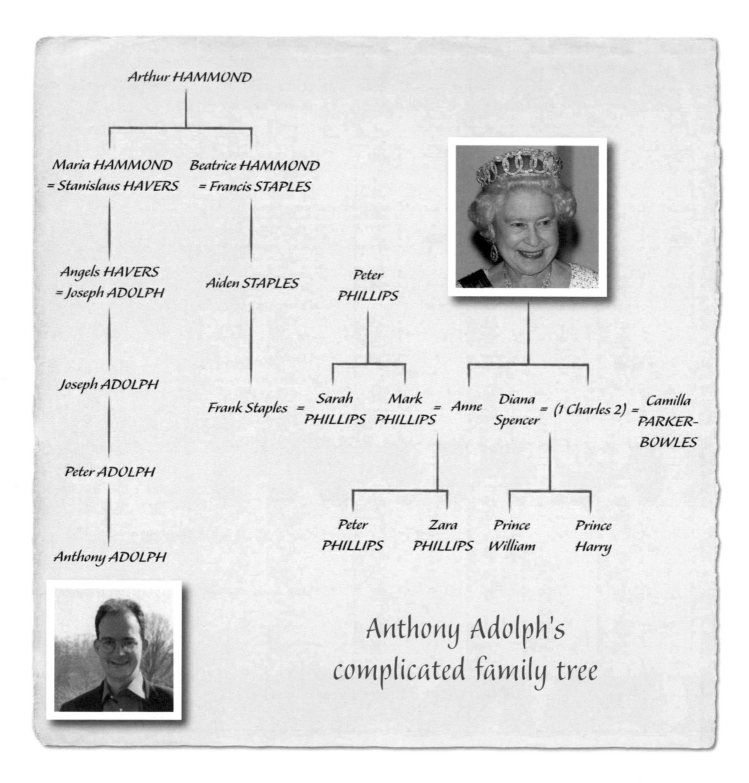

Arthur HAMMOND

Maria HAMMOND
= Stanislaus HAVERS

Beatrice HAMMOND
= Francis STAPLES

Angels HAVERS
= Joseph ADOLPH

Aiden STAPLES

Peter
PHILLIPS

Joseph ADOLPH

Frank Staples =

Sarah
PHILLIPS

Mark
PHILLIPS

= Anne

Diana
Spencer

= (1 Charles 2) =

Camilla
PARKER-
BOWLES

Peter ADOLPH

Anthony ADOLPH

Peter
PHILLIPS

Zara
PHILLIPS

Prince
William

Prince
Harry

Anthony Adolph's
complicated family tree

The Queen is my grandfather's second cousin's brother-in-law's mother-in-law – at least she was, before Mark Phillips and Princess Anne were divorced. But I can also say that my grandfather's second cousin's niece and nephew, Peter and Zara Phillips, are the Queen's grandchildren. My connection to Camilla Parker-Bowles is of course the most distant shown on this chart. I am Camilla's sister-in-law's ex-sister-in-law's husband's second cousin twice removed!

Complicated relationships

You can have great fun combining these terms to describe very complicated relationships. It's best to start by drawing up a family tree, keeping everyone on the right level. This chart shows one of the most interesting family connections I have found in over 25 years of tracing my family tree. My grandfather Joseph Adolph was a great grandson of Arthur Hammond. Arthur was also great grandfather of Frank Staples. This makes Joseph Adolph and Frank Staples second cousins. Frank Staples's grandchildren would be my fourth cousins, making Frank Staples my fourth cousin twice removed.

Look at the chart and you will be able to follow how these relationships work. Frank Staples married Sarah Phillips, sister of Captain Mark Phillips, who in turn married Princess Anne, daughter of Queen Elizabeth II. Frank Staples was therefore Mark Phillips's brother-in-law. Frank was uncle to Peter and Zara Phillips, the children of Mark Phillips and Princess Anne. When Mark Phillips married Princess Anne, he became the Queen's son-in-law, and brother-in-law to Prince Charles. Mark Phillips was therefore uncle to Princes William and Harry.

When Prince Charles married Camilla Parker-Bowles, Camilla became step-mother to Princes William and Harry. Camilla also became daughter-in-law to the Queen, and sister-in-law to Princess Anne.

Make a Family History Box

TIP

It's very good to have a spring clean and throw old things away, but please, don't ever throw out anything to do with your family tree. It is far too precious.

If it were not for old records, we would have a miserable time trying to explore our family trees. Keeping records safe is really important, and that goes for the ones you are now making yourself. Your family trees, Family History Forms, and everything else you make using this book, are part of your family records. In a hundred years time, people may be treasuring the notes you make today as valuable old records. But only if they haven't been thrown away. The best place to keep everything safe is in a special Family History Box.

1 Ask your parents if they have a spare cardboard box, or you could make one from cardboard yourself.

2 Paint your box. You could paint it a bright colour, or you could make it look like a treasure chest, with stripes of brown paint to look like planks of wood. You could even make a lock out of silver paper to go on the side.

3 Paint or write 'FAMILY HISTORY' on the lid.

4 Line the box with material to make it extra-special.

5 Put in everything you write down and collect, and keep it all safe.

5

Old Photographs: Making An Illustrated Family Tree

O pen the curtains, look through the window and look at the world. That's what we do every morning. Old photographs open windows too, but the world you see through them is very different to the one around us now.

Do you look like your ancestors?

While I was writing this book, I went to dinner in a house that had been built 180 years ago by my great great great great grandfather Perry Nursey. The current owners wanted me to tell them more about Perry, so I took along a picture of him. I was very surprised when they said 'you look just like him!'

When I looked at the picture carefully, I could see what they meant. Our chins and noses are quite alike. We have both lost some of our hair, but that could be a coincidence. Still, it gave me the idea of making the family tree you can see on page 52. I have a picture of each person in the line from me right back to Perry Nursey's mother, Catherine Fairfax, who was born in 1742.

My little collection has come about gradually, as a result of contacting different descendants of the Nursey family over 20 years. Some photos come from a cousin who lives at the back of Harrods in London. Another I found in an archive and the one of Rosalba was in the catalogue of an auctioneer, who had sold the original picture back in 1996. The final piece in the jigsaw, the picture of Jessie, was e-mailed to me by a cousin, quite by chance, while I was writing this book.

Perry Nursey as a middle-aged man

An illustrated family tree

Catherine Nursey
(1742-1827)
formerly Fairfax

Perry Nursey
(1771-1840)

Rosalba Howell
(1812-1895)

Jessie Waters
(1849-1935)

William Waters
(1875-1955)

Beryl Adolph
(1912-1994)

Peter Adolph

Rosemary Gale

Anthony Adolph

Natalie Lehain

Joanna Robinson

Do you think we all look alike?
Matthew, Ben and Thomas are
all quite young. But as they
grow older they are likely to
start looking more like their
grown-up ancestors.

Matthew Lehain

Ben Lehain

Thomas Robinson

Make an illustrated family tree

1 Collect pictures of each member of your family. Ask your parents if you can photocopy them, or scan and print copies on a computer. If this is not possible, you can always trace or copy pictures using paper and pencil.

2 Make the images so that they just show the heads and shoulders of each person. You could do this by cutting these out of copies of larger pictures, either as squares, circles or ovals. The pictures don't all have to be the same size, but the results will look better if they are. Please cut up copies: NEVER, NEVER cut original old pictures, as they cannot be replaced

3 Place the pictures on a large sheet of paper in the way you would arrange names on a family tree.

4 Once you have laid out all your pictures, stick them down gently with glue.

5 Write the names underneath each person, and draw lines connecting them together.

Below: The original photo

Right: A photocopy of the photo that can be cut and used in an illustrated family tree

Once all the faces are together on the family tree, you can really see whether or not you look like your relatives and ancestors.

A window on the 1890s: a Victorian family

My grandpa didn't have any old pictures of his family, but a few years ago I went to visit his cousin Cecil, who did. Cecil kindly gave me copies of his old pictures, and this is definitely my favourite.

Luckily, Cecil knew who everyone in the picture was, so we wrote their names on the back. My grandpa's father (my great grandfather) is the boy standing at the back, on the right. His name was Joseph too, and he was born in 1882. This picture was taken in 1896, so he was about 14.

The little boy sitting cross-legged on the left is Cecil's father, also called Cecil, who was born in 1892. He was about four when this picture was taken. He is wearing a 'sailor suit', a costume for young boys, similar to clothes worn by sailors at the time. Like all children then, he is wearing shiny boots, not shoes.

In 1896, Queen Victoria was on the throne, so this is a Victorian family. Victorian families were often quite big, and all those pictured are brothers and sisters, except for the lady standing at the back, who is their mother, Emily Adolph. She is my great grandmother. Her eldest child is Albert, who was born in 1878, and he is standing on the left. He looks terribly grown up, but boys tended to in those days. He's actually only 18. The youngest child is Monica, in the little white dress and frilly bonnet, sitting next to Cecil. She was born in 1893, so is about 3.

The smaller boy at the back is called William. He was born in 1885, so was about 11. He is wearing his school uniform, including a school cap. All schoolboys wore caps until around the 1980s. The older boys are wearing high white collars. These would have been starched, which means they were stiff, and not very comfortable to wear. They are all wearing quite a lot of clothing, and underneath they are probably wearing thick underwear called 'long johns', which had sleeves and legs, to keep them warm.

And just look at the mother's hat, covered with bows and feathers. Hats covered with what look like dead birds were very fashionable in the 1890s.

Albert

William

Emily

Joseph

Cecil

Monica

Family pictures
Portraits

Before photography was invented, the only way to show what people looked like was to draw or paint their portraits. Family portraits are now treasured family heirlooms, and sadly there aren't a lot of them around. It is always worth asking if any relatives might have old family portraits. I found two family portraits from the late 1700s, both owned by cousins of my grandparents, who very kindly let me take photographs of them.

This boy was called Thomas Mitchell Hammond, born in 1795 in Portsmouth, Hampshire. It was quite normal for young boys to have long hair then. He grew up to become a doctor in Brixton, London. I'm descended from his brother William.

This is Samuel Simpson, who was born in Little Bealings, Suffolk in 1777. He died in 1790, when he was only 13. My grandmother's cousin, who owns this portrait, told me a story about Samuel. He was very keen on horse riding, and one day a friend bet him that he could not jump a very tall hedge. Samuel tried, but fell off his horse and died. I'm descended from his sister Anne.

Black and white photographs

Photography was invented in 1826. Early photographs were very expensive and time-consuming to produce, so there are not many of them around. Henry Fox Talbot invented a quicker and cheaper way of creating pictures in 1839 and photography soon became very popular. Early photographs had no colour: they might be printed in black and white, or in 'sepia', which is brown and white. Sepia pictures often look warmer than black and white ones, and many Victorians preferred them.

Colour photographs

Colour photographs were invented in 1861. However, this process was tremendously expensive too, so very few were taken. Virtually all family photographs you will see up to the 1950s will be black and white, or sepia. In the 1950s, a way of creating cheap colour photographs was invented. Unfortunately, a lot, even from the 1980s, have faded badly – so your family are likely to look rather yellowish!

The tallest child in this old sepia photograph, above, is another great great grandmother of mine, Mary Ann Collingwood Paterson, known as Polly. She was born in 1854, so this picture was taken in roughly 1859. Her brother John James is wearing an 'Eton collar'. The smallest child, surprisingly, is their brother Robert, for back then boys wore dresses until they were 4 or 5.

This colour photograph was taken in 1915 by an inventor called Sergei Mikhailovich Prokudin-Gorskii. It is very unusual to find a colour photograph that is so old.

Digital photographs

You are probably more familiar with digital photographs, those that can be transferred from a digital camera onto a computer. This process was invented in 1969, but again was horrendously expensive. It was not until the late 1990s that digital cameras appeared that ordinary people could afford.

Labelling your family's photographs

Often, you will find old photographs that have no names or dates written on the backs of them. You might show them to your grandparents, and ask 'who is that?', but they may say 'we're sorry, but we don't know'. People seldom write on the backs of photographs because, at the time, it is absolutely obvious. You know who is in the photographs you have just taken, so why bother writing on them? The trouble is that, as time passes, we start to forget. I know a lady who has lots of old photographs of herself and her sister when they were little, but in some pictures she simply can't tell which of the two children in the pictures is her.

The solution is to write the names and dates on the back of your family's photographs now. If the pictures are your parents', ask their permission first, and do it in pencil, so you can correct mistakes. If you have digital pictures on the computer, you can click 'rename' and write a caption as the 'name' of the photograph.

It's best to use full names – forenames and surnames. Otherwise, in 50 years time, people will be asking 'that's Fred, but Fred who?' If you have lots of family photographs in an album, you can draw a family tree showing all the people who appear in the photographs. Stick this in the front of the album, so that in future everyone will know who was who. If the pictures are stored on the computer, you could scan the family tree and store the scanned image with them.

Above: 'Flapper' style from the 1920s
Right: Fashion from the 'swinging sixties'

How people change

1991

1945

1915

You are used to seeing your parents as grown-ups, and your grandparents as elderly people. It's just bizarre to think of them as young people, the same age as you, or actually younger.

Try to find pictures of your grandparents as they are now, and then as they were at different stages in their lives. I tried doing this with my grandfather Joseph Adolph, who I knew as a big old man with a white beard and a deep booming voice. He is shown here as a middle-aged man in 1945 (standing on the left) and as a little boy in 1915.

6

Of Mice, Dwarfs And Wizards . . .
Family History In Stories

Family histories are everywhere, not just in the real world, but also in the world of our imaginations. You may have come across family history in stories you have read. These are some of my favourites.

Family trees in *Harry Potter*

Whether you are a Pure-blood wizard, a Half-blood wizard or a Muggle (with no wizard blood at all) makes absolutely all the difference in the world of Harry Potter. Some wizards believe very strongly that only wizards of pure wizard ancestry should control the wizarding world. Others believe that you can be a wizard regardless of your ancestry. The Noble and Most Ancient House of Black's motto was *Toujours Pur*, which is French for 'Always Pure'. They supported Lord Voldemort's plan to kill off wizards who were not pure-blooded. J.K. Rowling drew a Black family tree going back 150 years. It contained new details about the family, which were key to guessing what was going to happen in *Harry Potter and the Deathly Hallows*, before it was published. She auctioned it for charity, and it sold for £30,000!

J.K. Rowling's own family tree gave her ideas for characters in *Harry Potter*. She adored both her grandfathers, Ernest Arthur Rowling and Stanley George Volant. They became Ernie and Stan, the two Knight Busdrivers who rescue Harry in *Harry Potter and the Prisoner of Azkaban*. But J.K. Rowling's grandmother Louisa Volant, who preferred her dogs to her grandchildren, gave her the idea for Harry's horrible 'Aunt Madge'.

Harry Potter, as played by Daniel Radcliffe in the films. J.K Rowling used some characters from her own family and a lot of imagination to create family trees for her *Harry Potter* books.

Hobbit family tree

J.R.R. Tolkien's story *The Hobbit* starts with Thorin, the Dwarf King, explaining his family tree to Bilbo Baggins, a Hobbit. Thorin's ancestor Thrain had found a wonderful mountain where he and his people mined fabulous jewels. But Thorin's grandfather, Thror, was driven away by a horrible dragon called Smaug. *The Hobbit* tells of the journey made by Bilbo, Thorin, Thorin's followers, and the wizard Gandalf, from the peaceful Shire all the way to the Lonely Mountain, to reclaim Thorin's throne.

Frodo the Hobbit as played by Elijah Wood in the films. Frodo had a very large family tree, and many of his relatives appear in the *Lord of the Rings* trilogy.

Hobbits, in case you do not know already, are small people, about half the size of adult humans. They have furry feet with leather soles (so they never wear shoes), and they live in holes called Hobbit Holes. They like nothing better than telling people how they are related to each other.

Another Hobbit, called Frodo Baggins, is the hero of Tolkien's next book, *The Lord of the Rings*. Bilbo sometimes calls Frodo his 'nephew'. Actually, Frodo was Bilbo's second cousin once removed on their fathers' side, and also his first cousin once removed on their mothers' side. Frodo's companions Merry and Pippin are related to him as well. Most Hobbits are usually related to each other several times over – and the more complicated the family tree, the better they like it.

An important human character In *The Lord of the Rings* is Strider. He is a tall, mysterious Ranger, from the wild lands beyond the Shire. He comes from a long line of Rangers, but before then his ancestors were something rather different. I can't say any more without giving away the story. Let's just say that who Strider's ancestors were proves very important to the story indeed.

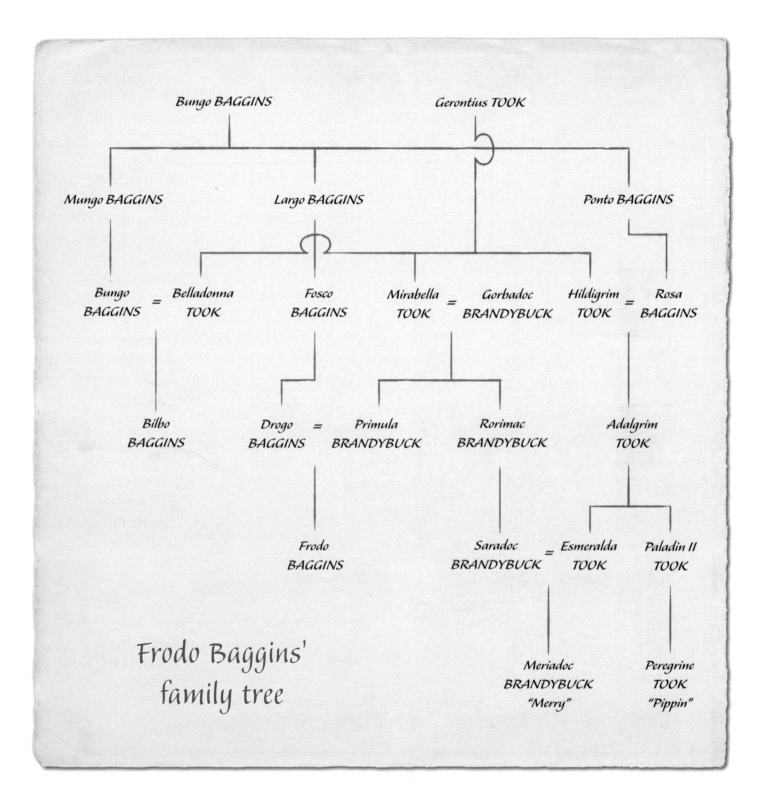

Frodo Baggins'
family tree

Find out more

You can look at some of the family trees I have mentioned here on the Internet. A good site for the family trees of Tolkien's characters is **http://www.tuckborough.net/**. Family trees of the Potters, Blacks and so on appear on **www.wikipedia.com** under 'Harry Potter'. Another amusing website gives a very big family tree of Mickey Mouse's friend Donald Duck: **http://duckman.pettho.com/tree/v_american.html** All of Donald's relatives shown here have appeared in Walt Disney cartoons over the years.

Frogs and Mice

The Ancient Greeks were so obsessed with family trees that they even made up ones for mice. *The Battle of the Frogs and Mice* is the story of Stealcrumb, a brave little mouse who goes to a pond for a drink and runs into the King of the Frogs.

'Who are you, stranger?', asks the frog. 'Where have you come from? Who is your father?'.

'I am called Stealcrumb', declares the mouse, 'and I am the son of an heroic father, Munchbread, while my mother is Lickmill, daughter of King Hamchomper. She bore me in the City of Cottage, and raised me on all sorts of delicious food, like walnuts and buns coated with sesame seeds and cheese…'

Later the frogs and mice fall out, and fight a great battle, which ends when they are both invaded by an army of crabs. Here is the mouse Stealcrumb's made-up family tree:

King Hamchomper
|
Munchbread = Lickmill
|
Stealcrumb

Draw an imaginary family tree

1 Try drawing the family tree of an imaginary family. They can be ordinary humans, or ones with special powers. They might be animals, like pigs, or chinchillas, or butterflies. They could be supernatural beings, like a family of giants or fairies, or even aliens – a whole family of orange spongy creatures with seven ears and three fleggiospongiolules (whatever they might be).

2 On your imaginary family tree, make up who the grandparents, great grandparents and so on may have been. You can also imagine future generations by adding the family's children, grandchildren – and so on.

3 Once you have drawn the family tree, pick two members of the family and write a small paragraph about their lives, their adventures, and their children.

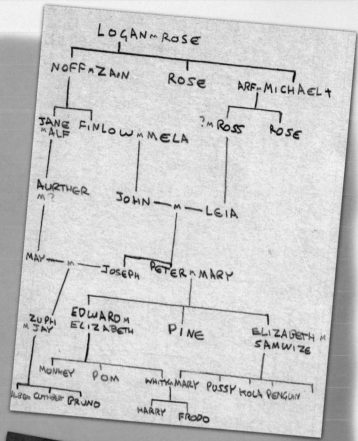

This family tree was drawn by me, for Bruno the bear, when I was 10 – proving that I have always wanted to be a genealogist. All the early names are made up, but the bottom two generations were all real toys that I had.

7

Where Do I Come From?

As you explore back through your family tree, you will find some families who stayed in one place for a long time, and others that moved about. Every story will be different. Part of the enjoyment of exploring family trees is to work out why people stayed put, or why they moved.

Why families move

War, slavery and adventure have all caused families to move around the world. The most usual reason for families moving from one place to another, however, was simply to earn a living. In the past, many people lived or worked on farms. A successful farm provided almost everything people needed – food, shelter, water from the well, wood for fires and tools, and hopefully some spare produce to sell. The trouble was that families grew too big for one farm to support. A farmer, his wife and five children could live happily on the farm. But what happened when those five children married and had five children each themselves? That's over 30 people already, to say nothing of their wives. Soon, some of the children would simply have to move away, to start a new farm or find work doing something else.

You often find families in which one child, usually the eldest (but sometimes the youngest), would remain in the parents' home, and the others would go to live somewhere else. In the 1500s, a farmer's son might walk to a nearby village and live there. But from the 1600s onwards, he could just as easily sail away to start a farm in a colony, such as north America.

In the 1700s, towns grew ever bigger, and included more and more factories. Here, many people could find work, not farming, but making things. Many also went to work in coal mines, the army, the navy, or as builders of new roads, canals, railways and houses.

Children whose parents have died are called orphans. Some English orphans emigrated overseas to start new lives at the Fairbridge Farm Schools in Australia. These children are starting their journey on an ocean liner, in 1948.

The people of Britain

Britain's population is a big mixture of people who have come here from somewhere else. In the last few decades, many people have come here from Eastern Europe, the Caribbean, Africa and Asia. Before then, for hundreds of years, immigrants came in small groups – Jews from Eastern Europe, black and Asian sailors and servants, traders from France and Germany, and many more, all intermarrying with the British people already here, and becoming ancestors of the modern British people.

But the earlier British were a big mixture too. Two thousand years ago, the Romans invaded Britain. They came from Italy, but their armies, called Legions, included men from all over the Roman Empire – from Germany, the Middle East and northern Africa, for example. There were Normans, who invaded England from northern France in 1066. The

Invaders of Britain

About six thousand years ago, farmers settled here. They came in tiny boats up the Atlantic coast, from north-west France, and before then from the Atlantic coast of Spain and Portugal. They were the people who first brought wheat and oats here to grow, and animals like sheep and cows. The people who were here before them lived by hunting wild animals. They had done so ever since they came here 10,000 years ago, at the end of the last Ice Age. They came here originally from France and Spain, where they had spent the freezing Ice Age living in caves – as cavemen.

All these people, Vikings, Romans, cavemen and the rest, intermarried with each other and became the ancestors of the British people.

Vikings from Scandinavia invaded eastern England and parts of Scotland, Wales and Ireland in the 8th and 9th centuries. The Saxons from northern Germany settled in England in the 4th and 5th centuries.

The travels of your ancestors

Once you have drawn a family tree, it's easy to see how your ancestors have moved about. Start with your parents, and think about where they lived, and what they did for a living. Then look at their own parents, your grandparents. Had the family moved? If so, try to work out why – or ask your parents if you don't know. By doing this you will start really understanding your family tree, and how things ended up the way they did.

Work often causes people to move about, but so too does retiring. Nowadays, when people grow old and live on old age pensions, they don't need to live near the office or factory where they worked. They can live wherever they want. Some old people chose to live at the seaside, and others move to live near their children and grandchildren.

Getting to know old family haunts

Before long, you will have quite a lot of places mentioned in your family tree. These places were home to different parts of your family. They were as familiar to them as your home is to you.

Old photographs will show you what these places were like. It's fun to research more about the places that your ancestors called home. In doing so, you will be able to understand more about their lives. For example, my father grew up in Falmouth, Cornwall, and became an engineer in the merchant navy. These two facts are linked. Falmouth is a port, and when he was growing up my father watched ships coming and going from all over the world. If he had lived near Heathrow airport he might have become an aeroplane engineer instead.

The earliest British people lived in caves like this one, shown left, which is at Inchnadamph in north-west Scotland. It contains bones of red deer, left over from suppers eaten by the first people who lived here after the end of the Ice Age.

Above: People today dressed as their Viking ancestors would have, a thousand years ago. *Far left:* a modern actor dressed as a Roman soldier would have been, two thousand years ago.

Make a star map, showing where your family comes from

1 Trace or photocopy this map of the British Isles. Mark the spot where you live now. Next to it, write its name, your name, and the names of your family who live with you.

2 On the map, mark other places in Britain where the rest of your immediate family live now. These may include your grandparents, uncles and aunts, and of course any of your brothers and sisters who have left home. If one or both of your parents do not live with you, mark where they live too. Label each spot with the names of the place, and of the relatives who live there now.

3 Using a coloured pen, draw lines to connect your home with everyone else's homes. The result will look like a star. Your star might just cover a small area – one village or town, for example. On the other hand, it may cover a lot of the British Isles.

4 Mark the homes of relatives or ancestors who have died. These can include any of your grandparents who may have died, great grandparents and any earlier ancestors you have discovered.

5 As before, write the name of the place, and of the people who lived there. Connect these spots to your spot with a coloured pen. Use a different colour to the one you used before. You could even use two coloured pens; one for ancestors on your father's side, the other for ancestors on your mother's side.

Make a star map, showing where in the world your family comes from

6 If you have relatives or ancestors overseas, then trace or photocopy the map of the world. Do the same thing as before, only this time your star might extend across the whole planet. Your Star Map will show how much your family has moved about.

7 It's fun to compare Star Maps with your friends. You can see how many of your friends it takes to cover the whole of the British Isles – England, Wales, Scotland, Northern Ireland and the Republic of Ireland. How many friends does it take to cover each of the world's continents – Europe, Africa, Asia, America and Australasia?

Finding Out About Where You Come From

Now that you've drawn your Star Map, you can find out
more about the places where your family used to live.

1 **At home** Ask your relatives what the places where they grew up were like. You can also do some research yourself. Your parents will probably have a road atlas, or other sorts of maps, on which you can find places where your family used to live. Most atlases have indexes of place names at the back. The main Google page (**www.google.co.uk**) includes a 'Maps' search engine that will show you anywhere in Britain.

2 **The library** Most libraries have a section for books on the British Isles and other parts of the world. Look in this section for books about the areas where your family lived, and see if they mention the actual places. What you learn here could be useful for your own family history. For example, if the place was well-known as a fishing port, or had a carpet factory, then maybe some of your ancestors were fishermen, or carpet-makers.

3 **The Internet** You can look the places up on the Internet and see what they are like now. If you type the place's name into a search engine like Google, you may find it has a website (usually designed to attract tourists). The site **www.visionofbritain.org.uk** lets you see old maps, and find out facts about different places in the past. If the place you're looking for is really small, you may have to search under the name of the nearest village or town. The website **www.genuki.org.uk** contains information on each county of the British Isles, and includes details about some of the parishes from old books.

4 **Out and about** If you're at a fête or fair, you might spot a stall selling old postcards. The postcards are often arranged by county. Looking through them, you will see what the county where your family used to live was like in the past. You may be lucky enough to find a postcard of the very place where your family used to live. You'll be luckier still if you could then persuade your parents to buy it for you; but you can always ask.

ACTIVITY

Draw a map of a town or village where some of your ancestors used to live.

1 Draw pictures of the houses where your family lived, and also other buildings that featured in their lives.

2 You could draw their school, where they worked, buildings such as temples, synagogues or churches where they worshipped, and the graveyard or crematorium where they were buried or cremated.

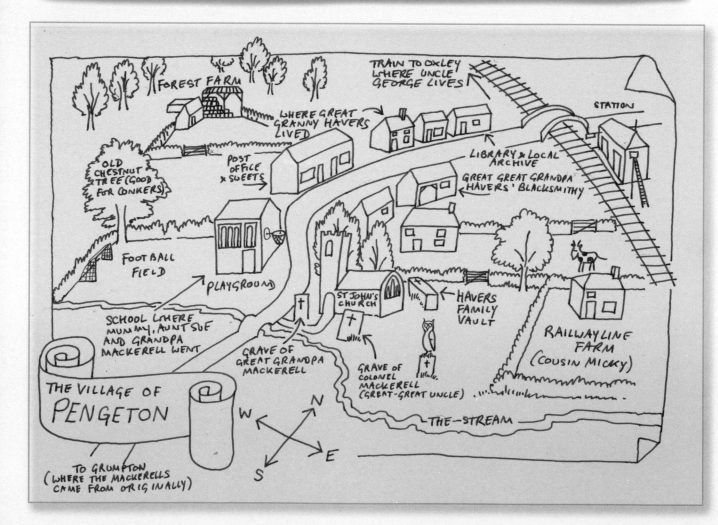

Ancestors from around the world: Princess Pocahontas

The early European settlers in North America quickly came into contact with Native American Indians, who had lived there since the end of the Ice Age. Princess Pocahontas (1595-1617) was the daughter of Wahunsunacock, King of the Powhatan people who lived in Virginia. When she was a little girl, her father captured one of the English colonists, John Smith. He was about to kill Smith, but the little princess begged her father to spare his life. Later, when the colonists' crops had failed and they were starving, Pocahontas persuaded her father to let them have some food.

Eventually, Pocahontas married one of the colonists, John Rolfe. She was baptised as a Christian, with the name Rebecca. In 1616, she and John Rolfe sailed to England, where she was introduced to King James I himself. The couple set sail to return to America, but while the ship was still in the River Thames Pocahontas fell ill, probably due to the effects of all the smoke in London, and died on 21 March 1617. She had had a life full of adventure, but she died aged only 21. She was buried by the Thames at Gravesend, where there is now a statue commemorating her. Pocahontas and John Rolfe had a son, Thomas Rolfe, whose descendants all carry Pocahontas's Powhatan Indian blood to this day. These include many of the richest white families in America, and the wives of two American Presidents, Woodrow Wilson and Ronald Regan.

Pocahontas' statue in St George's Church in Gravesend is a replica of a statue in Virginia, USA. It was a present from the Governor of Virginia to the British people.

Ancestors from around the world: John Ystumllyn

'It is the year 1748. The scene is the edge of an African jungle teeming with brightly coloured plants and alive with the cries of exotic birds and the almost deafening buzz of insects. An African woman is watching while her eight-year-old son creeps slowly towards a stream, his spear poised to kill a bird.

Suddenly, tall red-faced men emerge through the tangle of vines, their bodies covered in bright-coloured, alien-looking clothing. Thunderous booms and a smell of burning erupt from the end of the sticks they hold. The woman flees, but the boy cannot run. He stares wide-eyed at the 'devils', paralysed by terror. He feels hard, hot hands closing round his bare arms and sees the trees spin as he is hoisted up. The grief-stricken screams of his mother echo through the jungle as he is borne away towards the menacing roar of the ocean.'

This is how I imagined the capture of the real-life African boy who became John Ystumllyn. He was taken away in chains to a slave ship, but instead of having to work on the plantations of Jamaica, this boy became a personal servant to one of the ship's officers, who gave him the name John. He was taken to London, and sold to a Welsh gentleman called Ellis Wynn.

Ellis Wynn took John on a long journey, across England and into Wales, past the looming peaks of Snowdonia, until John saw the white crests of waves surging angrily against the Caernarvonshire coastline and the grey slate rooftops of the town of Criccieth. The coach then lurched down a track, with boughs of ash and blossom-laden hawthorn scraping against the sides of the carriage, until at last John saw his new home, Ystumllyn (pronounced Ist-im-lin).

Slowly, John learned to speak Welsh and English, and started working as a gardener. Nobody asked him his original name, so when he was baptised in the local church, the vicar wrote:

> 1756: John Ystymllyn (a Black), Servt. to Ellis Wynne of Ystymllyn Esqr., Novr. 16th.
>
> ('Servt' was short for 'servant')

The house in Wales where John Ystumllyn lived

John grew to love looking after the rambling gardens of Ystumllyn. Each lunchtime, a young maid called Margaret Gruffyd brought John's bread, cheese and beer to the garden. She was scared of the black-faced boy, for she had never seen a black person before. At first she would drop the food by the gate and run away. But soon she got used to him, and started talking to him, and John and Margaret fell in love.

Suddenly, Margaret was sent away to work in another town, so John ran away to join her. They set up home in a cottage, and had seven children. In those days, Welsh children were often given their father's first name as their surname. John's children were called 'son of John', which in Welsh is 'Jones'.

John was very happy, but sometimes people made nasty comments about his skin colour. Once, two girls asked him, 'is your blood black like your face?' John was very angry, and replied, 'you silly fools. You have white chickens and black chickens, but you know perfectly well they both have red blood!'

Three of John's children married, all to white people. Their children probably had brown skin, but after a few generations of marrying only white people, the descendants of John Ystumllyn became gradually whiter and whiter. I went to Criccieth a few years ago to look for them, but it was impossible to tell who was his descendant, and who wasn't. But I did learn that John is still well-known locally, because he is practically the only local character who was not born and bred in Wales. 'John Ystumllyn is dear to my heart!', one lady told me. Who knows – if she explored her family tree, she might find that she is descended from John herself.

Genghis Khan

I told you earlier how Prince William is descended, through his grandmother's grandmother, from Vlad IV of Valachia in Romania, the brother of the evil Dracula, who used to kill his victims with sharp sticks. Vlad lived in the 1400s. His family had ruled Valachia since the time of his own great great great grandfather, Basarab, the first Prince of Valachia. Basarab was a member of a fierce tribe called the Mongols.

The Mongols came from the cold, windswept steppes (plains) of Mongolia, between Russia and China. They were nomads, which means that they didn't have a fixed home. Instead, they rode around on their short, fast horses, attacking other people, stealing their food, clothes and money, and sometimes even making them slaves. They really were rather

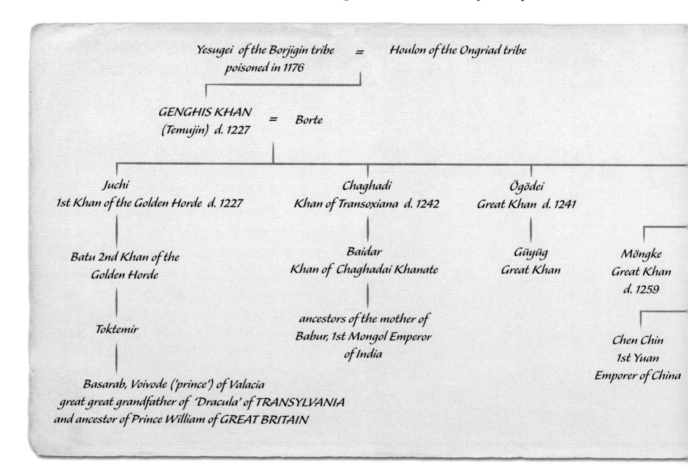

Yesugei of the Borjigin tribe = Houlon of the Ongriad tribe
poisoned in 1176

GENGHIS KHAN = Borte
(Temujin) d. 1227

Juchi
1st Khan of the Golden Horde d. 1227

Chaghadi
Khan of Transoxiana d. 1242

Ögödei
Great Khan d. 1241

Batu 2nd Khan of the
Golden Horde

Baidar
Khan of Chaghadai Khanate

Güyüg
Great Khan

Möngke
Great Khan
d. 1259

Toktemir

ancestors of the mother of
Babur, 1st Mongol Emperor
of India

Chen Chin
1st Yuan
Emperor of China

Basarab, Voivode ('prince') of Valacia
great great grandfather of 'Dracula' of TRANSYLVANIA
and ancestor of Prince William of GREAT BRITAIN

Genghis Khan's family tree

```
Tolui
d. 1233
   |
   +----------------------+
   |                      |
Kubilai Khan           Hülegü
Great Khan             d. 1265
d. 1294                   |
   |                   Abaka, Ilkhan of Persia
   |                   = Maria, daughter of
Temur Oljeitu          Michael VIII,
2nd Yuan               Emperor of
Emperor of China       Byzantium
   |                      |
   ↓                      ↓
Yuan Emperors          Ilkhans of PERSIA
of CHINA               (Iran)
```

fierce – certainly not the sort of people you'd want to bump into on the way home from school.

The Mongols' leaders were called Khans. In the late 1100s, their leader was a great warlord called Genghis Khan (d. 1227).

Genghis Khan was an ancestor of this same Basarab. Amazingly, this means that Genghis Khan is also an ancestor of Prince William.

Genghis Khan and his descendants took the Mongols' traditional raiding lifestyle to a new level by invading whole countries, including China, India, Russia and Romania. On the family tree of Genghis Khan's descendants, one branch were Princes of Valachia in Romania, another branch were the Yuan Emperors of China and a third branch were the ancestors (through his mother) of Babur, Emperor of India.

This makes Genghis Khan's family tree one of the most unusual and interesting in the world. Of course it also means he has absolutely loads of descendants all over the world. Prince William is only one of millions of people descended from Genghis Khan – you might even be another.

8

The Family Tree Of Life

Most normal family trees can be traced back only a couple of hundred years. But we all belong to a greater human family tree that can be traced back over 70,000 years. And humans are a branch of an even bigger one – the Family Tree of Life, that stretches back a mind-boggling 3.8 billion years, and includes all life – even your pet hamster.

The Human Family Tree:
Out of Africa

Wherever your family live now, you can be sure your ancestors lived in Africa about 80,000 years ago. New DNA science has proved what many people have believed for a long time, that we are all one big family. Some branches have gradually become white, and others black. We can draw a family tree showing how the different branches of the family tree all go back to the same ancestors.

All animals and plants are divided into species. Our species is called *Homo sapiens*, which is Latin for 'thinking man'. Our earliest *Homo sapiens* ancestors lived in Africa and were hunter-gatherers. We moved about in small groups or families, hunting wild animals, and collecting fruit, nuts, eggs and anything else we could eat. The people most similar to them now are the San people (or Bushmen) of southern Africa, a descendant of whom is the former South African president Nelson Mandela.

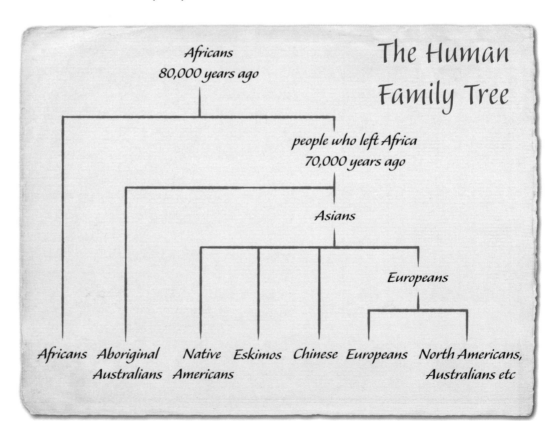

The Human Family Tree shows how we all descend from people from Africa.

France
Maman

Spain
Mamá

USA/UK
Mom/Mum

India
Maji/Ammee

Greece
Mana

Russia
Mat

Japan
Haha

Brazil
Mãe

How did they speak?

We do not know the names of our ancestors who lived 80,000 years ago. But children now generally call their mothers 'mama', 'mum', or 'mummy'. Similar words are used by children all over the world. It is likely that these words all come from a word for 'mama' that our ancestors used in Africa, all those years ago. Although more than 2,300 generations have passed, each generation, including you, were babies, who grew up as little children calling their mothers something like 'mama'.

Africa and beyond

About 70,000 years ago, a tiny group of these people left Africa, and wandered into the Middle East. They split up, and went in different directions. Some wandered along the coastline, around India and down the Malaysian peninsular, crossing the sea in primitive boats to reach Australia. They are the ancestors of the Australian Aborigines, some of whom still live as hunter-gatherers, just like their distant ancestors.

Other people who had left Africa went east through Asia, becoming ancestors of the people there, including the Indians and Chinese. Some went up the north-east of Asia and crossed into what is now Alaska. Some of these travellers remained in the frozen north, becoming ancestors of the Inuit (Eskimo). Others went south, spreading through north and south America. They are the ancestors of the Native American tribes of north America, like the Sioux and the Apaches, and also of the South American peoples like the Incas and the Aztecs.

Ice Age Ancestors

Other people stayed in central Asia and started moving west. About 30,000 years ago, some of them ventured into northern Europe. Europe was gripped by the Ice Age, a

period when the weather was very much colder than it is now. These people hunted animals like mammoths, which were enormous elephants, with thick, woolly fur to keep them warm. The hunters would eat the mammoths' meat and cut up their thick fur skins to make clothes. People also lived in caves in the mountains, and sometimes decorated the walls with paintings of the animals they hunted. For this reason, we call them 'cavemen'.

About 10,000 years ago, the weather got warmer. The ice melted and the mammoths died out. The people who lived in Europe came out of their caves and hunted smaller animals like deer and wild boar in the forests. Their descendants are the British, the French, the Spanish, the Germans and the other people who live in Europe.

As we saw in the last chapter, people have been moving all over the world since then, in armies, on ships, or just individual people making journeys on their own. This means that members of all the different branches of the human family have intermarried, time and again.

DNA

We know about the human family tree thanks to DNA. DNA is short for 'deoxyribonucleic acid'. It exists inside every cell in our bodies. It is DNA that tells our bodies how to grow. Your DNA determines what colour hair and eyes you have, and also more important things, like how many legs and arms you have. DNA is passed down from parents to children. Usually, it is passed on unaltered, but sometimes it is passed on with a tiny change. These changes are then passed on to later generations. Everybody whose DNA contains a particular change must have the same ancestor. By studying the differences between people's DNA, scientists can work out how people are related to each other. By studying DNA in people all over the world, scientists have worked out how all the branches of the human family tree are connected.

The Family Tree of Life

We have said that our ancestors lived in Africa 80,000 years ago. There were not very many humans beings alive then – perhaps no more than a few thousand. We wore no clothes, and built no houses, but we could make fires and stone tools, like arrowheads, and knives. We spoke to each other, told stories, sang songs, and laughed and cried, just as we do now.

Modern humans evolved from earlier types of human, such as *Homo erectus*, who were similar to you and me, only a bit hairier, and with smaller brains. Your great great great (etc) grandparents, about a million years ago, were *Homo erectuses*.

They evolved from ape-like *Australopithecuses*, who were much smaller and hairier, and they in turn had evolved from smaller, ever more furtive creatures. Going back about 60 million years, our ancestors were tiny tree shrews, with very strong little arms and legs with toes and fingers that clung to the branches of trees. If you think about it, we're not all that different to them: anyone who enjoys climbing trees, nibbling nuts and fruit and curling up in nice warm beds (or nests) will understand exactly what I mean.

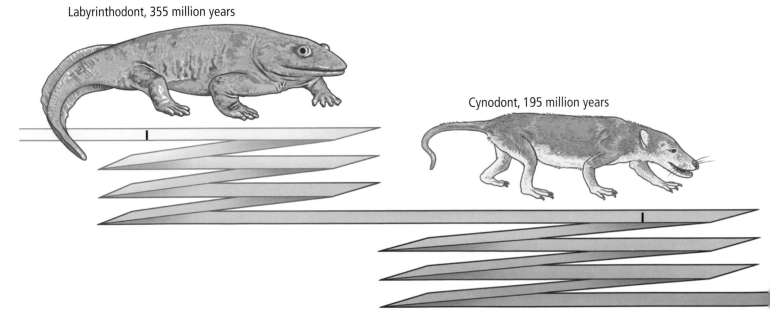

Labyrinthodont, 355 million years

Cynodont, 195 million years

Tree shrews had ancestors, of course, for the 'magic rope' of ancestors stretches back across almost unimaginable amounts of time. When dinosaurs roamed the Earth, our ancestors were tiny furry creatures, no bigger than a pound coin, called *Hadrocodiums*. All mammals, from us to horses, dogs and cats and gerbils and elephants, are descended from these miniscule ancestors – it was because they were so small that they avoided being eaten by dinosaurs.

Hadrocodiums were the smallest survivors of a family called *Cynodonts*, who flourished before dinosaurs came along. *Cynodonts* were fierce creatures with murderously sharp teeth, but this didn't stop the dinosaurs eating most of them in the end.

Our *Cynodont* ancestors evolved out of *Labyrinthodonts*, who lived about 355 million years ago. They are our ancestors, and also the ancestors of all mammals, reptiles, birds and

If you live near London and want to see some *Labyrinthodonts*, go to Crystal Palace Park, where you can see several of them lounging around the shore of the lake. They happen to be models made out of concrete, because real *Labyrinthodonts* don't exist any more – though of course we, their descendants, are alive and well.

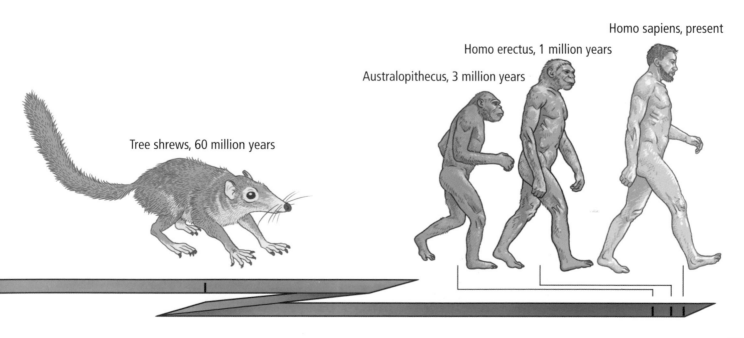

Homo sapiens, present

Homo erectus, 1 million years

Australopithecus, 3 million years

Tree shrews, 60 million years

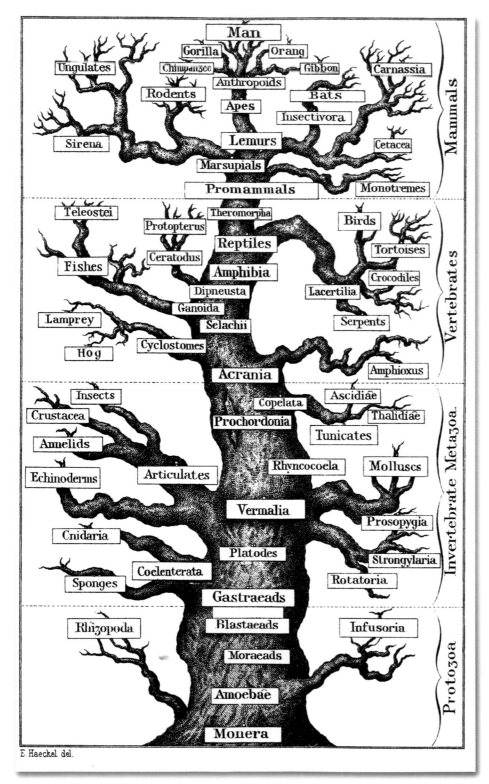

E. Haeckel del.

It is possible to draw a family tree where, instead of people's names, you can show how species are related to each other. This is called a Family Tree of Life. The first one, shown left, was drawn by German scientist Ernest Haeckel in 1874.

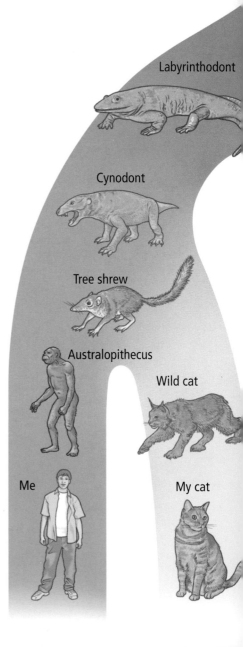

Labyrinthodont

Cynodont

Tree shrew

Australopithecus

Wild cat

Me

My cat

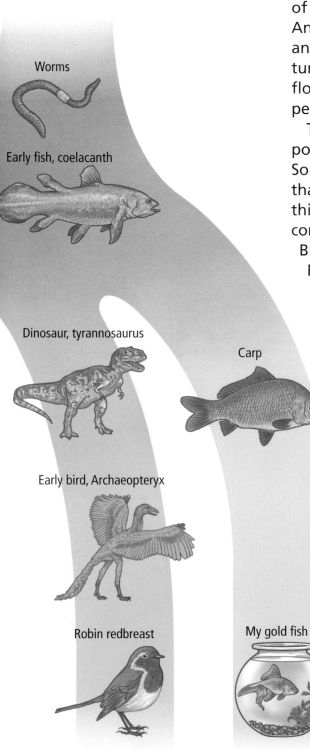

Worms

Early fish, coelacanth

Dinosaur, tyrannosaurus

Carp

Early bird, Archaeopteryx

Robin redbreast

My gold fish

This Family Tree of Life shows
how we are related to some
other species

amphibians. Their own forebears were fish, who crawled out of the water on their strong fins, that then evolved into legs. And fish came from worm-like creatures that swam the ancient seas, and they from tiny, jellyish creatures, who in turn evolved from creatures that had just one cell each, and floated about, unable to see, or hear, or think, but probably perfectly happy in their own way.

This takes us back to about 3.8 billion years ago. At that point, for reasons we don't yet fully understand, life began. Some people believe that God created life, and others think that it developed naturally out of the warm seas. Others think that the first miniscule living things came here on a comet from a distant planet. We don't know which is true.

But I do know that the first tiny, living things on planet Earth were your and my great great great (etc) grandparents. They were the living creatures with whom our family tree started. All living things on Earth belong to branches of the same family tree.

This means that you are closely related to other humans. You are a bit less closely related to monkeys and apes. Other mammals, like horses, lions, hedgehogs and moles are a bit further removed, but they are still your cousins. You are more distantly related still to the birds, lizards and crocodiles, then frogs and fish, then worms, seashells and insects. You are very distantly related to the trees and flowers. Just think of it: even the potatoes from which your chips are made grew on plants that are very, very, very remote cousins of yours.

Draw your own personal Family Tree of Life

You can draw your own personal Family Tree of Life, like the one on pages 86-87, connecting you to other living things around you.

1 Choose a pet, if you have one, or the birds and animals you see out of the window.

TIP

You can find out more about *Labyrinthodonts, Cynodonts,* and look at more pictures of what scientists think they looked like, on the Internet. You can draw pictures of them on your Family Tree of Life

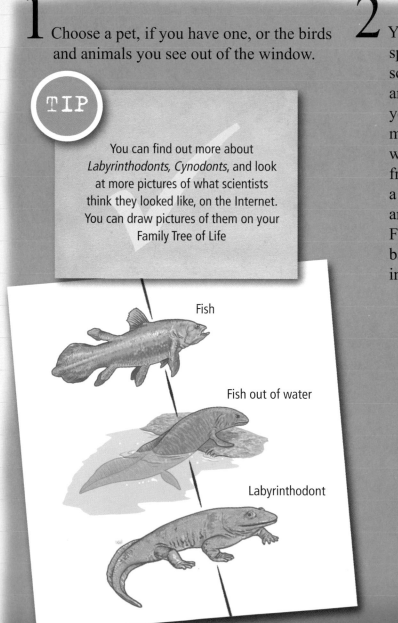

Fish

Fish out of water

Labyrinthodont

2 You don't have to show every single species in the family tree. In many cases, scientists are still trying to work this out anyway. But you can show generally how you are related. If you have chosen a mammal like a cat or hamster, then you will show how you are both descended from *Hadrocodiums*. If you have chosen a bird, then you need to show how you are both descended from *Labyrinthodonts*. For a goldfish, you need to trace right back to the fishy ancestors you both have in common.

You will notice how, although these animals are all quite different to each other, they also have many similarities. They all have two eyes, for example. We have two legs and two arms, yet you know that you can walk about on all fours if you feel like it. Your arms were once the forelegs of animals like *Cynodonts*. Before then, they were the fins of our fish ancestors. By looking at these pictures, you will see how one type of creature could evolve out of another, resulting eventually in that very special creature – you!

Fossils are the key

Scientists have been working out the family tree of life for the last 300 years. They are helped by fossils, which are the remains of ancient creatures found preserved in rocks. Fossils help us work out what distant ancestors of ours, like the *Cynodonts* and *Labyrinthodonts*, looked like. Charles Darwin (1809-82) worked out that all life on Earth had evolved from tiny living things. Evolution means that families of plants or animals change very slowly over long periods of time, so as to suit the environment in which they live. When they explore our distant past, scientists like Darwin act as genealogists, working out our family tree and tracing back to our earliest ancestors.

Our distant 'Hobbit' cousin, *Homo floresiensis*.

Neandertals and 'Hobbits'

Our ancestors about 1 million years ago were *Homo erectus*. Some of these evolved into us, but others evolved into different human species. During the bitterly cold Ice Age, some evolved into tough, hairy people called Neandertals. Neandertals were our distant cousins, but sadly they died out about 25,000 years ago.

Other *Homo erectuses* ended up on a tiny island between Australia and Asia, called Flores. Here, they gradually became smaller and smaller, until they were only about three feet tall. Their bones were only discovered a few years ago. They were about the same size as Hobbits, the little creatures made up by J.R.R. Tolkien in *The Lord of the Rings*. So scientists nicknamed the tiny people of Flores 'Hobbits' too, though their official scientific name is *Homo floresiensis*, which is Latin for 'man of Flores'. Sadly, these little cousins of ours died out about 12,000 years ago.

Some animal family trees: Mewers

This creature pictured below is Kobalt Kid, which didn't suit him, so I used to call him Mewey Pooey, which most certainly did. He mewed almost constantly, especially at night. He was born on 14 April 2001 and belongs to a breed of cat called the Maine Coon. They are called that because they come from Maine in the United States, and look a bit like furry racoons.

Many types of domestic animal, such as horses, cattle, dogs and cats, are bred very carefully. Their owners allow them to mate only with the best examples of animals of the same breed. They are called 'pedigree' animals because their family trees are recorded, and they are often given very elaborate names. Mewey Pooey's pedigree certificate shows that his father was called 'Champion Guldfakse's Harold Blue Tooth', and his mother was called 'Peconic Clyternnestra'. The certificate records all Mewey Pooey's grandparents, great grandparents and even his great great grandparents. Cats can give birth to kittens when they are only a year old themselves, so it's hardly surprising that Mewey Pooey's great great grandparents weren't born all that long ago. His father's father's father's father was called 'G.C. Mount Kittery's Penobscot', and was born on 5 March 1986.

You may think it odd that mewers have great great grandparents who were born a mere 25 years ago. But imagine being a hamster.

Hamsters

There are several types of hamster, but the most common is the Golden Hamster. Golden Hamsters are found in pet shops, classrooms, family homes and laboratories all over the world. Have you ever thought about their family tree? Where do they come from? Are they all related?

Golden Hamsters come from Syria, which is in the Middle East, between the Mediterranean Sea and Iraq, but they are extremely hard to find. An elderly female hamster was caught there in 1839, and brought back to England. Later, a few hamsters arrived in London in 1880, and their descendants lived there until 1910, when they died out.

In 1930, a zoologist (someone who studies animals) called Israel Aharoni set out to find some more. He heard stories of Golden Hamsters living near a Syrian village, and asked the local sheikh for help. The sheikh told the villagers to help Aharoni, and together they started digging a hole in a nearby field. Hamsters in the wild have very deep burrows, to keep them safe from the heat, predators and, I suppose, hamster-collectors. Eight feet down, Aharoni found a tiny burrow, containing a very annoyed mother hamster and eleven tiny babies. Aharoni carefully picked them all up, and took them away.

As you know, hamsters like nothing better than escaping from their cages, and this family were no exception. Several squeezed out of their cage and scurried away almost at once. Of the remaining ones, several managed to gnaw through the floor of their wooden box and scuttled back to the wild. Soon, only four young hamsters remained.

Unlike humans, it is perfectly natural and normal for hamsters to mate with their brothers and sisters. Hamsters can start having children when they are only three months old, and pregnancy, which takes us humans nine months, takes hamsters only 16 days. Soon the hamsters were producing children, and then grandchildren and great grandchildren appeared. Within a year, the family already consisted of 150 little Golden Hamsters.

In 1931, a friend of Aharoni's smuggled a few of the hamsters into England in his coat pockets. From these small beginnings come all the Golden Hamsters in Britain.

Did you Know?

Aphids breed so rapidly that some are actually born pregnant. If you tried tracing an aphid's family tree back over just one year you might find it had more than 300 generations of ancestors!

9
Family Trees Through Time

Family trees connect us back to the past. They remind us that history didn't just happen to other people – it happened to our ancestors, and it affected the way our family trees developed. Your family tree might connect you to people who were affected by history, or even to people who made history by their acts and deeds.

Personalising time

Time is a very big, confusing thing, that has existed for vast eternities. We have tried to make it less confusing and frightening by dividing time up into units, like minutes, hours, days, months and years. Scientists estimate that the universe is about 13.7 billion years old. This is a huge number, but at least we know what a year is, so all we have to do is imagine 13.7 billion of them. But even numbers are faceless and nameless.
The earliest ways by which our earlier ancestors measured time were a bit friendlier, because they used names.

King lists

The ancient Sumerians lived in what is now modern Iraq, 5,000 years ago. They invented the cuneiform writing we looked at earlier in this book, on page 13. They also drew up 'King Lists', showing a sort of family tree of the kings who had ruled since the dawn of time, which they thought was about 450,000 years earlier. This was made up, of course, because modern humans, let alone kings, didn't even exist so long ago. The point is that by dividing 450,000 years' worth of time up into the names of imaginary kings, the Sumerians made that huge amount of time seem a lot less frightening.

Queen Victoria's long reign lasted from 1837 to 1901, a period called 'the Victorian era'.

Royal timekeeping

You might think that things have changed since the Sumerians – but think again. Whether an object, or a house, was made in the 1840s, or a great great grandfather was born in the 1880s, you might say they were from the 19th century. But you can also say they were Victorian, because Queen Victoria was on the throne at the time. The 1500s (the 16th century) is often called the Tudor period, as the Tudor family were on the throne, just as the Stuart dynasty gave their name to the next century, the 1600s. The 18th century is usually called the Georgian period, because for most of the time the throne was occupied by George I, George II and George III. So, just like the Sumerians, we use the family tree of our royal family to give names to periods of time.

94

Timeline, 1800-present

This will help you see how your family history fits into wider historical events from 1801 onwards.

TIP

For events before 1800, see the excellent interactive timeline on the BBC's website,
**http://www.bbc.co.uk/history/british/
launch_tl_british.shtml**

Your Family Events

The Battle of Waterloo in June 1815, at which the British (in red) defeated the French (in dark blue).

1801	England, Scotland and Ireland become the United Kingdom
1805	Battle of Trafalgar: Admiral Nelson defeats the French at sea
1807	Abolition of the trade in slaves in the British Empire
1815	Battle of Waterloo: end of the war between Britain and Napoleon's France
1820	Death of George III: his son George IV becomes king
1825	First steam train passenger service
1826	*Burke's Peerage*, recording the family trees of lords, first published
1826	First photographs
1829	First police force created (in London)
1830	George IV dies and is succeeded by his brother William IV
1837	Births, deaths and marriages start being recorded in England and Wales (before then there were parish registers) from 1 July

1837	William IV dies and his niece Victoria becomes queen	
1838	Slavery abolished altogether in the British Empire	
1841	First census taken on Sunday 7 June: censuses have been taken every 10 years since (except 1941, because of the Second World War)	
1840	First postage stamps	
1845	Potato Famine in Ireland: many Irish people flee to England, Wales and Scotland, and abroad, looking for food	
1847	First public park (at Birkenhead near Liverpool)	
1849	Cholera epidemic, spread by dirty water, kills 33,000 people in Britain	
1851	Census taken on Sunday 31 March	
1855	Births, deaths and marriages start being recorded in Scotland from 1 January	
1854-1856	Crimean War between Britain and Russia	
1858	All wills start being proved centrally, rather than in local bishops' courts	
1859	Charles Darwin publishes *The Origin of Species*, his theory that we evolved from ape-like creatures	
1861	Census taken on Sunday 7 April	

First Postage Stamp: The Penny Black, the first true postage stamp. It was issued in 1840, when the young Queen Victoria was on the throne, so it has a picture of her head on it. All British stamps ever since have shown the ruling king or queen's head.

1864	Births, deaths and marriages start being recorded in Ireland from 1 January (though marriages of Protestants had in fact been recorded in this way since 1845)	
1867	First animated film	
1871	Census taken on Sunday 3 April	
1880	All children aged 5-10 have to go to school	
1881	Census taken on Sunday 4 April	
1885	Invention of motor car and motorbike	
1887	Stapler invented by Henry Heyl: gramophone invented by Emile Berliner	
1891	Census taken on Sunday 6 Apri	
1892	First colour photographs	
1893	All children aged 5-11 must go to school.	
1893	First wireless (radio)	
1894	First stuffed toy bear (they were called 'teddy bears' from 1902)	
1899	All children aged 5-12 must go to school.	
1899-1902	Second Boer War between British and Dutch settlers in South Africa	
1901	Census taken on Sunday 31 March	
1901	Queen Victoria dies and is succeeded by her son Edward VII	

The motorcycle was invented in 1885, and first went on sale in 1894. As you can see, the early ones really were simply motorised bicycles.

A lovely old teddy, from 1902.

		Your Family Events
1901	First vacuum cleaner	
1903	First aeroplane (flown by the Wright Brothers) – but unfortunately the first parachute was not invented until 1913	
1908	Kenneth Grahame writes *The Wind in the Willows*	
1908	Olympic Games held in London	
1908	Old Age Pensions introduced	
1909	First Chinese restaurant in Britain opens in London	
1910	Edward VII dies and is succeeded by his son George V	
1911	Creation of Society of Genealogists, encouraging everyone to explore their family trees	
1911	Census taken on Sunday 2 April (later censuses were taken, but are to be kept secret until 100 years after they were created)	
1912	Ocean liner 'Titanic' hits an iceberg and sinks	
1912	Creation of the Royal Flying Corps, later to become the Royal Air Force	
1914-1918	First World War between British and German allied groups: this sees the first tanks, poisoned gas, and conscription (whereby all young men were forced to join the armed forces). British Allies win	

Terrified survivors flee from the sinking Titanic in the freezing cold waters of the North Atlantic.

		Your Family Events
1917	Revolution overthrows the Russian Tsar and introduces Communism in Russia	
1918-1919	Terrible outbreak of Spanish flu kills about 250,000 people in Britain	
1918	All men over 21 and women over 30 allowed to vote	
1919	First woman (Lady Astor) elected to Parliament	
1921	All children aged 5-14 must go to school	
1921	Ireland divided into Northern Ireland, and semi-independent southern Irish state called Eire (Eire becomes fully independent in 1949)	
1926	A.A. Milne writes *Winnie the Pooh*	
1926	Logie Baird invents television	
1927	Creation of the BBC	
1928	First cinema film with sound	
1928	Voting for all men and women over 21	
1928	First appearance of Walt Disney's Mickey Mouse	
1928	First sliced bread	
1930	Arthur Ransome's *Swallows and Amazons* published	
1936	J.R.R. Tolkien's *The Hobbit* published	
1936	(January) George V dies and is succeeded by his son Edward VIII	

A.A. Milne named Winnie the Pooh after a teddy bear owned by his son, Christopher Robin Milne.

The idea of selling bread that was already sliced is an American one: the first sliced bread was produced commercially by Otto Rohwedder in Missouri in 1928.

		Your Family Events
1936	(December) Edward VIII stops being king by abdicating and is succeeded by his brother George VI	
1939-1945	Second World War, between Britain (and allies) against Hitler's Germany and Japan. All young men forced to join armed forces. Many cities bombed from the air on both sides. Many city children are sent as 'evacuees' to live with families in the countryside for safety. Food was rationed severely. First Nuclear bomb used against Japan. In 1945, The Allies win the war.	A soldier throwing a hand grenade in the Second World War.
1940-1945	Winston Churchill (Conservative) is Prime Minister	
1941	First true computer	
1944	Free Secondary Schools	
1945	Tove Janssen's first Moomin book (*The Moomins and the Great Flood*) published	
1945	Creation of the United Nations	This huge machine is a single, very early computer created in 1946, called the Electrical Numerical Integrator and Computer ('ENIAC').
1945	Clement Atlee (Labour) becomes Prime Minister	
1947	India becomes independent from Britain	
1948	The ship *Empire Windrush* brings the first post-war immigrants from the Caribbean to Britain	
1948	National Health Service created, with free health treatment for everyone	
1948	Olympic Games held in London	

1949	Publication of Enid Blyton's first *Noddy* book	
1949-1954	C.S. Lewis writes the *Chronicles of Narnia*	
1951	Winston Churchill becomes Prime Minister again	
1952	George VI dies and is succeeded by his daughter Elizabeth II. Many people buy television sets for the first time so as to watch the coronation live	
1953	Discovery of DNA	
1954-1955	J.R.R. Tolkien's *The Lord of the Rings* published	
1955	Start of ITV	
1956	Britain's first nuclear power station	
1955	Anthony Eden (Conservative) becomes Prime Minister	
1957	Harold Macmillan (Conservative) becomes Prime Minister	
1957	Unmanned Russian Satellite 'Sputnik I' goes into orbit	
1958	First motorway	
1963	First computer mouse	
1963	Sir Alec Douglas-Home (conservative) becomes Prime Minister	
1965	Harold Wilson (Labour) becomes Prime Minister	

Nuclear Power – Britain's first nuclear power station, Calder Hall, Cumberland, opened in 1956.

The M1 in 1967, with far less traffic than today.

1965	End of the death penalty: all serious crimes punished by prison, not hanging	
1965	Start of comprehensive schools	
1966	*Star Trek* first shown on television	
1966	England wins football World Cup	
1969	U.S. Space ship Apollo takes men to moon for the first time	
1970	Voting age reduced to 18	
1970	Edward Heath (Conservative) becomes Prime Minister	
1971-1997	Conflict in Northern Ireland between British troops and the IRA	
1971	First e-mail	
1971	Pounds, shillings and pence replaced by modern decimal money	
1972	Many Indian families expelled from Uganda by Idi Amin come to Britain	
1973	All children aged 5-16 must go to school	
1973	Britain joins the European Economic Community (now called the European Union)	
1974	Harold Wilson (Labour) becomes Prime Minister	
1976	James Callaghan (Labour) becomes Prime Minister	
1979	Margaret Thatcher (Conservative) becomes first woman Prime Minister	

Margaret Thatcher, Prime Minister of Great Britain from 1979 to 1990.

Personalising the Timeline

1 Look at the dates written on your Family History Forms.

2 Using a pencil, write events that took place in your own family in the blank space next to the Timeline. If your grandmother was born in 1935, write the year, and her name next to the closest date that I have provided.

3 As you learn more about your ancestry, you can add more details to the Timeline (it might get quite crowded, but that doesn't really matter – time is a pretty crowded thing).

| 1930 | Arthur Ransome's *Swallows and Amazons* published | |
| 1936 | J.R.R. Tolkien's *The Hobbit* published | 1935 Anne Jones (Granny) born |

Some family trees are affected directly by events on the Timeline. This is my great great great great grandfather Michael Lawrence Mason. He was a doctor in London at the time of the terrible outbreak of cholera in 1849. 13,000 people died in London, and poor Dr Mason was one of them, as the note on the reverse of this old portrait card shows.

Case study: Related to a witch? Draco Malfoy's magical past

Tom Felton has become famous as one of the actors in the *Harry Potter* films, in which he plays the wicked young wizard Draco Malfoy. As reported in a number of newspapers, when Tom explored his family tree, he had a real surprise, because he found links back to people in the 17th century who were genuinely connected with witchcraft.

Witches and warlocks, who practise magic for good or evil, are made up. But in the past plenty of people thought they were real. Sometimes innocent people, who were just a bit peculiar, or who suffered from fits, might be accused of being witches. Some were put on trial, and were executed for their supposed crimes.

A panic about witches took place in Salem, Massachusetts, America in 1692-1693, just over 300 years ago. One of Tom's relatives, Lieutenant Nathaniel Felton, was a witness at the trial of two young girls in Salem, Massachusetts. The girls had suffered from fits, and people thought they were witches. Nathaniel Felton was a witness on the side of these poor girls, but could not stop them being found guilty of witchcraft.

Also in Tom's family tree, on the same Felton side, was John Proctor. John saw what was happening, and realised that everyone had gone mad. He tried to make people realise how stupid they were being, but his reward was being accused of witchcraft himself. John was hanged for this 'crime' on 19 August 1692.

We know that John was not a witch. Yet the fact remains that Tom Felton, who has become famous for playing a fictional wizard, is actually related to people who were once thought to possess magic powers, just over 300 years ago.

Past and Present

Sometimes, family trees can link you to the past in surprising ways. For actor Tom Felton, family trees reveal an extraordinary coincidence, and they had a massive effect on how the Stuarts and Radcliffes lived and died too.

Doomed Dynasties I: The dissatisfied Stuarts

It's good to explore your family tree, but sometimes family history can bring misery, or even death.

The Stuart family were Kings of Britain until James II was overthrown in 1685. He fled into exile in Paris, France, taking the Crown Jewels with him. His son James 'the Old Pretender' and grandson Charles 'the Young Pretender' grew up on the Continent, but led very frustrated lives. Instead of enjoying life abroad, they were both obsessed with regaining the throne that they thought was rightfully theirs.

In 1715, 'the Old Pretender' organised an uprising in northern Britain, but it was crushed rapidly by the government. In 1745, his son 'the Young Pretender' organised a larger rising in Scotland, unfurling the royal standard and proclaiming himself 'King Charles III'. He is better known by the name his Highland supporters gave him – 'Bonnie Prince Charlie'. His rebellion almost succeeded, but his army was defeated by the government at the Battle of Culloden in 1746. He fled back to the Continent, and died as a disappointed, fat, drunk old man in 1788.

The last Stuart left was Bonnie Prince Charlie's younger brother Henry. Henry was more realistic, and accepted that he would never become king. Just before he died, he sent the Crown Jewels back to London, and thus ended a family struggle that had lasted over a hundred years.

James II

Cardinal Henry Stuart, the last of the exiled Stuart dynasty.

Doomed Dynasties II: the Romantic Radcliffes

The Stuarts' rebellions affected many other families. The Radcliffe Earls of Derwentwater joined the 1715 and 1745 rebellions out of loyalty to the Stuarts, who were their close cousins. In 1715, the Earl really did not want to go to war, but his wife embarrassed him by crying 'If you won't join the rebellion, give me your sword and I'll go instead!' The Earl went, but was captured, taken to the Tower of London, and beheaded. His wife knew it was all her fault, and her ghost is said to haunt their home, Dilston Castle, to this very day.

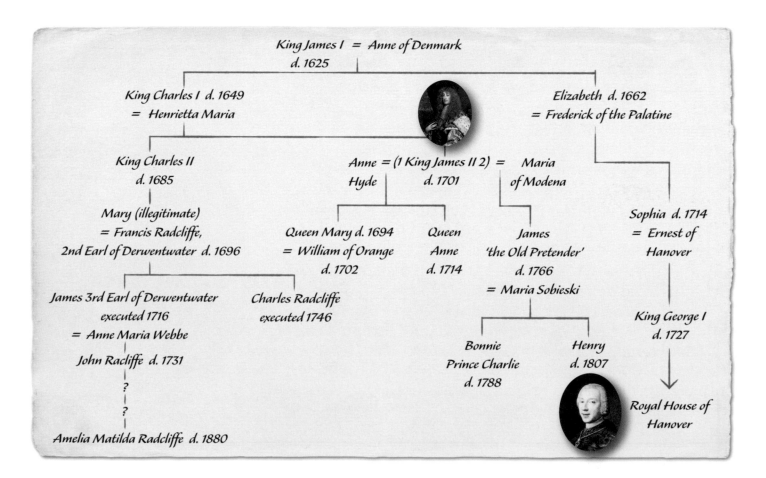

King James I = Anne of Denmark
d. 1625

King Charles I d. 1649 = Henrietta Maria

Elizabeth d. 1662 = Frederick of the Palatine

King Charles II d. 1685

Anne = (1 King James II 2) = Maria of Modena
Hyde   d. 1701

Sophia d. 1714 = Ernest of Hanover

Mary (illegitimate) = Francis Radcliffe, 2nd Earl of Derwentwater d. 1696

Queen Mary d. 1694 = William of Orange d. 1702

Queen Anne d. 1714

James 'the Old Pretender' d. 1766 = Maria Sobieski

King George I d. 1727

James 3rd Earl of Derwentwater executed 1716 = Anne Maria Webbe

Charles Radcliffe executed 1746

Bonnie Prince Charlie d. 1788

Henry d. 1807

John Racliffe d. 1731

?
?

Royal House of Hanover

Amelia Matilda Radcliffe d. 1880

In 1745, the Earl's younger brother rode off to support his cousin Bonnie Prince Charlie. He too was caught and sent to the Tower of London. You can guess what happened next – CHOP!

Over a hundred years later, a mysterious woman appeared at the ruins of Dilston Castle, claiming to be Amelia Matilda Radcliffe, the only surviving descendant of the doomed Earls. She said the castle was hers, and started hanging family portraits on the crumbling walls. When the authorities came to tell her to leave, she threatened them with an old sword that she said had once belonged to the Earls. They took the sword away, but she then sat down very grandly in an old chair, and simply refused to move. In the end, they just picked up the chair and carried it out with Amelia still sitting in it, protesting loudly.

Stubborn Amelia was so obsessed with her family's past that she spent the rest of her life insisting she was the true heir of the Earls of Derwentwater, who had lost everything through their loyalty to the doomed Stuarts.

Both James and Charles Radcliffe were executed for fighting on the side of their Stuart cousins. They died here, at the Tower of London. It is open to the public, so you can visit the Tower yourself.

10

Life In The Past

Exploring your family tree takes you on a journey back into the past. It opens windows on the way our ancestors used to live. The way we live has changed a lot even just in the last hundred years.

Your grandparents will have seen many things coming into existence that we now take for granted. You'll be amazed how much they can tell you about the way even quite ordinary things have changed. Mobile phones, iPods, and the Internet had never been thought of when they were little. They will be able to tell you a lot about what their homes and schools were like. They may be able to remember great events like the Second World War.

Write the story of an ancestor

'Biography' is the word we use for writing down someone's life. A biography can be a couple of lines, or a big fat book. Once you have heard about your grandparents, and maybe great grandparents and even earlier ancestors, you will have a jumble of information about what they did, where they were from and what happened to them. It's interesting then to sit down and try writing their lives.

1 You can base your biography on the person's Family History Form. Start at the beginning: write when and where they were born, and who their parents were.

2 Write where they went to school, what they did for a living, when and where they married, who their children were, what they did when they retired.

3 If they have died, write when and where this happened.

4 Hopefully, you will have heard stories about them. You can include these, at the appropriate time.

An example of a family story

My grandmother was scared of mice. In 1939, when the Second World War broke out, my grandfather joined the army. One day he was at home, wearing his uniform, which included a revolver. My grandmother screamed, because she had seen a mouse scuttling across the carpet. My grandfather calmly took out his revolver, took aim, and shot the poor mouse dead. Writing my grandfather's biography, I would include this story after he got married (1936) and before the story of what he did in the War (1939-45).

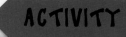

5 You are likely to find, through doing this, that there are gaps in your knowledge. You might find, for example, that you've absolutely no idea what grandma did between leaving school and getting married. You can make a list of questions to ask next time you see her, or if she has died you can ask her children instead.

The Timeline in chapter nine will help you add details to your ancestors' biographies. It will give you new questions to ask your parents and grandparents. If your grandmother was born in 1935, then these events took place just after her birth:

1936	J.R.R. Tolkien's *The Hobbit* published
1936	(January) George V dies and is succeeded by his son Edward VIII
1936	(December) Edward VIII stops being king by abdicating and is succeeded by his brother George VI
1939-1945	Second World War, between Britain (and allies) against Hitler's Germany. All young men forced to join armed forces. The Germans bomb many cities in what was called 'The Blitz'. Many city children are sent as 'evacuees' to live with families in the countryside for safety. Food was rationed severely. In 1945, Britain wins the war

So, you could ask:
Did you read The Hobbit *when you were little?*
Do you remember George VI being on the throne?
Do you remember the Second World War?
Were you an evacuee?
Was your father a soldier?
Was anyone in your family killed in the war?
Did you experience bombing?
Did you ever wear a gas mask?
What was it like having rationing?

6 You will realise quickly how much people's lives were affected by their parents. If children moved from one place to another it was probably because their parents had changed jobs. Children's choices of career were often determined by what their parents did. So the next step is to write the biography of the parents. And when you do that, you will find that their lives were affected by their parents – and so on right back along the 'magic rope' of ancestors.

7 You can write the answers on the back of that person's Family History Form, and perhaps write a longer biography, based on the new information you have learned. Your family history investigations will show how each generation's actions affected the next generation down. Your work will not only record what they did, but it will also start explaining how and why your family came to be the way it is now. You can add detail to your ancestor's biography by asking questions and doing some background research yourself.

Imagine having to queue up outside on an icy morning in order to go to the loo!

Forget fitted bathrooms and nice hot showers: in great grandpa's day, having a bath generally involved climbing into one of these metal bathtubs and using water heated on the fire.

Life At Home

One thing you can ask your parents and grandparents about is what the homes where they grew up were like.

All about loos

You take it for granted that your bathroom and loo are indoors, and probably nice and warm. This has only been common since after the Second World War (1939-1945). Before then, many people had a tin bath that was placed in front of the fireplace in the living room, filled with water heated in buckets and kettles on the fire. This involved so much work that often several members of the family would get in one after another, usually starting with the grown ups and ending (in rather dirty water) with the children.

The rich used to have indoor loos, but without plumbing. The contents had to be emptied outside by servants. The less wealthy had a loo in a little brick hut in the garden. Outside loos had no heating, and in very cold winters the water in the loo might freeze. The poor (i.e., most people) had to share one loo between several families. It was only after 1945 that many families started converting their houses to create an indoor loo and bathroom, but those who could not afford to carried on as before, some until the 1980s.

How many rooms?

You might have to share your bedroom with some of your brothers or sisters. Where possible, parents try to give their children separate rooms, or at least to provide bedrooms that are not too crowded. Until the early 1800s, people thought differently. Even if someone had quite a big house, they would still expect all their children to share one room. This could result in 10 or more brothers and sisters all squashed into the same room. Several children might share one bed. They would 'top and tail'. This means that one child would lie one way, and the next the other, so that your head would be next to your brother or sister's feet. In the 1850s, if there was space, the Victorians started allowing one bedroom for their daughters, and one for their sons (and they thought that was being rather generous).

Having to share beds wasn't always bad news. These children, in an 1866 painting by Frederick Daniel, are using it as an opportunity for a Midnight Feast!

Questions to ask about home

Questions you can ask your parents and grandparents about the way they lived can include:

Where did you live?

How many rooms did your home have?

Did you have your own bedroom?

Did your family have a car (or, if the person is very old, ask 'did your family have a horse?')

Did you have an outside loo?

Did you have a tin bath?

What was the garden like?

What games did you play at home?

What were your friends called?

Life at School

Your great great grandparents probably went to school, just as you do, but school life has changed a lot over the years.

In the 1800s, all towns and many villages had schools. Most were run by churches. Schools were usually bitterly cold, with small, high windows to stop children from gazing out of them. I don't know whether you like school meals now, but I can assure you they were worse in the past. When I was at school in the 1970s we had to eat stew full of lumps of fat, mashed potato made out of powder, and lumpy custard. If you didn't eat it all, you had to sit looking at it while all the other children were let out to play.

Leaving school early

Until less than 50 years ago, many children left school as soon as they could because their parents needed them to go out to work, to bring in much-needed extra money. Between 1870 and 1880, the government started forcing children aged 5 to 10 to go to school. The age at which children were allowed to leave has risen steadily since then. It rose to 11 in 1893, to 12 in 1899, to 14 in 1921 and to 16 in 1973. In 2007, the government discussed raising it to 18, perhaps by 2013.

Very few children had any choice over their futures. Most would simply do the same as their parents. Sons of vicars and lawyers might become vicars or lawyers. Sons of craftsmen like carpenters or blacksmiths would learn their father's trade. The children of factory workers would go to work in the same factory. Fishermen's sons would go to sea with their fathers and their daughters waited on the quay-side to clean and gut the fish when the boats came back. Some boys might decided to join the army or navy instead (but then again, a lot of soldiers' and sailors' sons became soldiers and sailors too).

Until the mid-1800s, most poor children did not go to school. Many worked in mines, like this boy.

This 1879 painting shows the naughtiest boy in the class having to wear a dunce's hat as a punishment.

Questions to ask about school

Questions you can ask your parents and grandparents about the way they lived can include:

Where did you go to school?

Did you have a nickname?

What were your school friends called and what were their nicknames?

What subjects did you study at school?

What were school meals like?

What uniform did you wear?

What were your teachers called, and did they have funny nicknames?

What examinations did you pass?

Did you go on to further education, such as university or an apprenticeship?

Nasty punishments

Teachers used to be much stricter than they are now.

Children could be beaten if they were naughty, or late, or even just being sulky.

Boys were caned on the bottom. Girls were caned across their hands or legs. Children who could not learn their lessons had to stand in the corner wearing a big pointed hat, with 'D' for 'Dunce' on it. Dunce is an old word for 'idiot'.

My old Latin master used to pick up children who weren't concentrating by the hair on the back of their necks, which was extremely painful.

School Photographs

Schools often let a profes-
sional photographer come
and take portrait pictures of
their pupils, for the parents
to buy. These often end up
in family albums, or in the
loft. Here are two, one of a
Scottish boy called Kenneth
taken in about the 1950s,
and one of me at Nursery
School, taken about
1971. Below is a team phot-
graph from 1924, showing
my grandfather.

Aunt Sissy
With love from
Kenneth

Christmas
Term

George's College Bantam Team.
Xmas, 1924.

Left to Right: A. van Zeller, C. Parker, J. O'Dowd, E. van Zeller, M. Dreaper, J. Adolfh, W. Mitchell, R. O'Brien.
Front Row: C. Ryan, P. Dowden, F. Conolly, M. Lucie-Smith, A. Ronegialli, J. Dunn, P. Lesnor.
Rev.ᵈ P. Alexander.

This was probably taken in Scotland in around the 1920s, but sadly nothing has been written on the back so we do not know any more about the master and his pupils. The big white collars some of the boys are wearing are called Eton Collars. They were held onto the shirt with little studs, and were often starched to make them stiff. They could be incredibly irritating to wear, as the stiff edge of the collar could rub on your neck and make it sore.

If you know where your ancestors went to school, you might find that the school still has pictures of them. There are often photographs of the whole school, and also of people in school plays, or on school trips.

Special Days
Birthdays

When you explore family papers, you might find photographs of your family's birthday parties. These pictures may well include relatives who are not alive any more, who you can add to your family tree. Ask your parents and grandparents what they remember about their birthdays when they were little. What presents do they remember being given? Did they have birthday cakes? Were they given 'the bumps' at school? Remembering people's birthdays can be very difficult, so some people make a list of the names and dates, or write them on a calendar or in their diaries, or keep a Birthday Book.

Balloons, party hats, and wearing your best clothes are all part of the traditional way of celebrating birthdays that we inherit from our parents.

Did you know?

Some people have more than one birthday a year. The Queen has two- her real one on the 21 April, the day she was born, and an official one on 17 June so that people can celebrate in nice sunny weather.

Birthday Books

A Birthday Book is a special book with an entry for each day of the year, in which you can note friends' and relatives' birthdays. I find the only trouble with birthday books, though, is you forget to look in them at the right time. But old birthday books, or other lists of birthdays, are very useful, because they can be used to add exact dates of birth to your family tree.

A tradition passed down in many families, generation after generation, is for parents to give their children birthday cakes. Your family may have some old photographs like this, showing the birthday boy or girl blowing their candles out. It is considered good luck to blow all the candles out in one puff – a task that becomes harder the older you become, and the more flames there are to extinguish. There is one candle in the cake for each year the child has been alive, so in the picture on the left we can tell that this is the boy's fourth birthday. You may be able to work out the ages of people in your family photographs in the same way.

Make a Birthday Book

If you haven't got a Birthday Book, you could ask for one as a birthday or Christmas present. Or you could make one yourself.

1 Take three sheets of A4 paper and a sheet of cardboard the same size.

2 Fold them in half.

3 Staple them together down the fold, or pierce holes in the fold and tie the pages together with a ribbon to make into a book.

4 Write 'BIRTHDAY BOOK' on the cover, and your name, and decorate it however you want, perhaps with a drawing of your family.

5 Birthday Books are arranged like diaries, with a small space for each day of the year. At the top of each page, write the months of the year – 'JANUARY' at the top of the first page, 'FEBRUARY' at the top of the second, and so on.

6 Drawn a line down the middle of each page. Write half the dates of the month down the left hand side of the page, and half down the line at the centre.

TIP

Don't forget that the months have different numbers of days – 31 in January, March, May, July, August, October and December, and 30 in all the rest except February, which has 28 normally, and 29 in leap years, so include numbers 1-29. Don't write days of the week, as these change from year to year.

MARCH

1
2
3
4   17
5   18
6   19
7   20
8   21
9   22
        23
        24
        25
        26
        27
        28
        29
        30
31

7 Fill in the birthdays of your family. If your sister Yasmin's birthday is on 4 April, write 'Yasmin' in the slot for that day. Think of the future, when your great grandchildren might find it, and wonder who everyone was. So it's better to write 'Yasmin Jansson' (if that was her surname), plus her year of birth, and also write 'my sister'. That way, people in the future will find the information more useful and interesting.

8 You can also fill in the birthdays of ancestors who have died. That way, for one day each year, you will be able to remember and think about each of your ancestors.

Hallowe'en

Ask your parents and grandparents if they celebrated Hallowe'en and if they have any old photographs of them doing so.

For thousands of years, the people of Britain, Ireland and the other lands that lie along the roaring coast of the Atlantic celebrated a festival called Samhain, pronounced 'sow-ain'. The scattered members of each tribe would come together in their sacred places, marked by standing stones, or the burial mounds of their ancestors. They would decide how many of their cows and sheep they could feed with hay and oats during the winter, and would kill the old and weak animals, so as to enjoy a great feast. They would light great bonfires, and sing songs to honour the declining sun, bidding him to return, reborn and strong again, in the spring. And they remembered their ancestors, whose cold bones lay in the burial mounds near their homes.

After the British Isles became Christian, one and a half thousand years ago, some old beliefs faded away, but others continued. People now believed the old burial mounds were gateways to an underground realm, where the dead lived, together with the mysterious fairy race, the Tuatha de Danann. On the evening before Samhain, the ancestors and the fairies would ride forth, taking possession of the world of the living for one night – the Night of the Dead. Samhain is 1 November, which Christians celebrate as the day of All Saints, or 'All Hallows' in old language. So the Night of the Dead became 'All Hallows' Eve', or Hallowe'en. The bonfires and fireworks of Guy Fawkes Night, which is celebrated on 5 November, have their origins in the ancient fires of Samhain as well.

Many people celebrate Hallowe'en now by carving scary faces into pumpkins

Diwali

If your family is Hindu, Jain or Sikh, you probably celebrate Diwali, the Festival of Light, at the end of Autumn. Diwali is at the end of the Hindu month of Ashwayuja, which usually falls at the end of October or early November.

Diwali, like many other festivals in the autumn and winter (including the Christian Christmas) is a time of coming together for families and friends. Your parents and grandparents may have photographs, cards and happy memories of past Diwalis.

Diwali marks the end of autumn, when the world takes a gasp before the first winter snows start flurrying down from the tall peaks of the Himalayas. Hindus believe that Diwali commemorates Rama, the king of Ayodhya in north-east India. Rama's story is told in the Hindu epic poem the *Ramayana*, which relates how he defeated the demon king Ravana, 'he of the terrifying roar'. Rama went away from his city for 14 years, and lived a humble life in the forest. Then, when he came back to Ayodhya, his joyful people lit rows of lamps to celebrate his return. The Hindu for 'rows of lamps' is *deepa-wali*, so the festival is called Deepawali, or Diwali.

Above: the forces of good and evil battle it out in an illustration from the *Ramayana*.
Right: Hindus light lamps at home to celebrate diwali.

Summer holidays

Maybe your family will have many memories and pictures of summer holidays. Now, many people go abroad for their summer holidays, because travelling in aeroplanes is quite cheap. Your parents may have taken you to the Mediterranean, or even further afield.

Before the 1970s, air flights were extremely expensive. Most families stayed in Britain, and went on holiday to seaside towns like Blackpool in Lancashire and Brighton in Sussex.

In the 1800s, most working people only had a few days off work each year. Their seaside holiday might be a single day-trip, made by train or in a horse-drawn coach, crammed full of family and friends.

Games to play on the beach around 1905 included this one, shown above — Leapfrog.

This is what most people's summer holidays were like in the past. On the back of this photo it says 'Seaford, Sunday, Aug. 5th 1928, Joe splashing my legs, Angela holding me, taken by Joe Junior with A's camera'. Imagine the wash and hiss of the waves going in and out over the pebbles, and the seagulls crying overhead, and what the family may have been saying — 'did you get us all in, Joe?' or 'This water's very chilly!'. If you use your imagination, this photograph is a time-machine, that can transport you back to a scene in a family's life, a long time ago.

Questions you can ask your parents and grandparents about the way they lived can include:

Did you go away on holiday in the summer?

How long were the holidays?

Did your family go on holiday with any relatives?

What activities did you do on holiday?

Shanklin, on the Isle of Wight, was a popular holiday resort when the above picture was taken in about 1914. You can see the lift that brought people down from the hotels on the cliffs, and the horse and carriage taking people to the station. On the beach are beach huts, where people would change into their swimming costumes.

In Victorian and Edwardian times swimming costumes, as shown on the left, were very different to those we wear today and covered most of the body.

Old money

In 1971, Britain's money was changed to the decimal system, where a pound is worth 100 pence – ten 10p pieces make a pound. It's pretty easy to work out. Before 1971, our ancestors had to struggle with a much more complicated system of coins, that dated back to Anglo-Saxon times. They used pounds, shillings and pence. There were 20 shillings to the pound, and 12 pennies to the shilling, so there were 240 pennies to the pound. The system was referred to as 'LSD', using the Latin words *Libra*, 'pound', *Solidus*, 'shilling', and *Denarius*, 'penny'. Something costing one pound, four shillings and two pence was written £1-4-2, or £1/4/2, or £1'4'2. All very complicated.

Most older people will be able to show you a few pre-decimal coins that they have tucked away. These may include sixpences – coins worth six pence – that some mothers still keep to put in Christmas Puddings.

Questions to ask about money

Some older people feel that money is a private matter, not to be talked about. You should ask your parents and grandparents if they would mind talking about money. If they say yes, you could ask:

How much pocket money were you given?

Did you have a job (such as delivering newspapers) while you were at school, and if so how much were you paid?

What were you paid for your first job?

If you bought a house, when was that, what did it cost, and how could you afford to pay for it?

In the World Wars

The First World War was fought between 1914 and 1918, and the Second World War between 1939 and 1945. The first war was also called the Great War, because at the time nobody could imagine a worse one following.

Both were between Britain and Germany, though they involved many other countries all around the world, that joined one side or the other. In both wars, Britain's main allies included Russia, France and the United States. Many men from all over the British Empire, including Canada, the Caribbean, New Zealand, Australia, India (which then included what is now Pakistan), and parts of the Far East and Africa also fought on the British side.

Much of the fighting took place in Continental Europe (such as France, Belgium and Italy), north Africa and parts of Asia. Huge numbers of soldiers were killed or wounded. Other men and women, such as doctors and nurses went to help them, and some of these were killed too. The Germans also flew over Britain, first in airships and then aeroplanes, dropping bombs on the cities. Consequently, many people were killed in Britain too.

The 'Home Front'

In the Second World War, air raid wardens were appointed in every parish to watch out for German bombers. They sounded an air raid siren, a horrid, wailing noise that warned everyone to take shelter. The wardens would sound the siren again when the raid was over, and clear areas where unexploded bombs had dropped. Some 200,000 people volunteered to be wardens, including many women, such as my grandmother, Mrs Maureen Rietchel, who is pictured here in 1937 with her eldest daughter, Ann.

These wars seem distant to us now, but your grandparents may well have been children during the Second World War. They would lie in bed, terrified that German Nazis might attack their homes, worrying about their fathers who were in the army, and perhaps actually hearing the drone of German aeroplanes overhead, and the explosion of bombs. There was a true spirit of bravery in those times, though. Instead of showing how frightened they were, many British people tried to joke about it all, and carry on with normal life, come what may.

War memorials

The people who were killed fighting in the First and Second World Wars are remembered on war memorials. These are stone plaques or pillars, inscribed with the names of those who died. Look out for them in town squares, village greens, parks and churchyards. The more you look, the more you will see – showing you just how many people were killed. The many soldiers who were killed fighting abroad are also named on war memorials at battlefields in those countries. These pictures are of a war memorial at Gallipoli, Turkey. British troops and allies from Australia, New Zealand, France, Canada and India tried to capture this area from the Turks (who were on the German side) in 1915. They failed, and 140,027 of them were killed – an enormous number. Every single name on the memorial commemorates a life that was lost.

In these pictures, Scott Crowley (right) has just found the name of his great uncle, James P. Crowley (top, in his uniform). Scott is 34: James was only 24 when he was killed and is commemorated on this memorial.

A family at war

You might think that members of the same family were usually on the same side in wars. The First World War was a horrible example of just the opposite, because the rulers of Britain, Russia and Germany were all very closely related. Nicholas II of Russia and George V of Britain were first-cousins, because their mothers were sisters. In addition, George V, Kaiser Wilhelm II of Germany and Nicholas II's wife Alexandra were all first cousins of each other, because each was a grandchild of Queen Victoria. Their family tree is on page 28. Before 1914, they all used to meet up for parties and picnics. Unfortunately, each ruler thought that family ties were less important than what they believed were the best interests of their own countries. Germany and Britain became bitter enemies in 1914, and it was jolly lucky for Britain that Russia decided to join in on the British side.

Two soldiers off to war posing with their friends and relatives at Knightswood Barracks, Glasgow, Christmas Day 1914 just before they set off to fight the Kaiser in what became the First World War.

Medals

You might be shown old papers to do with the wars, or medals that were given to your ancestors. If you can find out what these medals are, they will tell you a bit about where and when your ancestors served. Many medals were awarded over the years. The commonest for the two World Wars are:

First World War

- 1914 Star, for soldiers (and some sailors) who fought in France and Belgium between August and November 1914.
- 1914-15 Star, for all servicemen (army, navy etc) serving abroad in 1914 and/or 1915.
- British War Medal 1914-20, for everyone who served abroad during the War.
- Victory Medal, given to most people who served in the war.

Memorial Plaque or Death Penny, given to families who had lost someone fighting in the War.

Second World War

- 1939-45 War Medal, for anyone who served 28 days or more in the war.
- 1939-45 Star, for everyone who served overseas.

TIP

You can identify others using guides to medals, such as William Spencer's *Medals: The Researcher's Guide* (National Archives, 2006), available in libraries, or ask a specialist medal dealer.

British War Medal (1914-20)

1939-45 Star

On the postcard:

POST CARD

dence

Address

_...f H Company's fellows
...n the ground is a Channel
...the one I am resting on is Irish
... English. Observe the beautiful
...round about. We drill_

Postcards from the front

A group of young soldiers in the First World War (1914-18) had the picture above taken and printed on a couple of postcards, so they could each send a copy home to their families. One writes 'Some of H Company's fellows. The one on the ground is a Channel Islander, the one I am resting on is Irish, the other is English. Observe the beautiful country round about. We drill ankle deep in mud. Yours sincerely, James H. Petrie'. 'H Company' was the name of their division of the army regiment in which they served. When James calls the countryside 'beautiful' he is making a joke to keep his spirits up, for it is indeed mud, mud, mud as far as you can see – and probably very cold too.

A boy in his uniform, off to fight, and quite possibly to be killed. If so he would have been one of the 19 million people killed in the First World War.

Heritage Museums

Museums can seem boring if they have nothing to do with you. But if you go to a heritage museum thinking about what it can tell you about your own family, it will become very interesting indeed. A room made to look as it would have done in, say, 1900, can tell you a lot about how your great great great grandparents may have lived.

Many local museums have fascinating displays showing what life was like in the past. Some even contain reconstructions of rooms as they were, a hundred or more years ago. If there is such a museum near you, ask whether you can visit it.

A visitor comes face-to-face with a magnificent replica Anglo-Saxon helmet in the Sutton Hoo museum in Suffolk, where you can discover how our ancestors lived and died in Anglo-Saxon times.

A crofter's life in Skye

Colbost Folk Museum on the Isle of Skye shows exactly what life was like for many crofters (small farmers) in Scotland until very recently indeed. This picture shows a typical 'blackhouse', built of local stone, with rocks tied to the thatch to stop it blowing away in vicious winter storms. The blackhouse was divided into two rooms. One was for the family, who snuggled into a single room with only one bed, and a fire in the middle. No washing machines or deep freezes here! The other room was for the animals, particularly the cow who gave them milk. Sharing your house with cows sounds unpleasant and smelly, but actually they helped make the place much warmer in winter.

11

Names, And What They Really Tell Us

Everyone has a name, and most people have two or three. We all take this for granted – but just imagine for a moment what life would be like without them. If it were not for names, it would be completely impossible to identify each other. We would not be able to explore family trees, or to talk about our ancestors. Just imagine the confusion.

Looking up your Surname

By finding out what the surnames in your family mean, you can learn something about your ancestors who lived almost 1,000 years ago, when surnames started becoming fixed.

What does your name mean?

You can explore the meaning of first names and surnames using special dictionaries. Your local library should have at least one. You can have fun translating your names (and your friends' names) into modern English. For example:

Andrew Purcell: Andrew means 'warrior' in Greek and Purcell is old French for 'little pig', so the name Andrew Purcell literally means 'warrior piglet'.

Phoebe Cubitt: Phoebe means 'bright' in Greek and Cubitt 'elbow', so Phoebe Cubitt means 'bright elbow'.

Thomas Knight: Thomas is Aramaic (an old Biblical language) for 'twin', and Knight is Old English for a 'child', so Thomas Knight means 'twin child'.

Vincent Todd: Vincent is from a Latin word meaning 'conquering' and Todd is Old English for a fox, so Vincent Todd means 'conquering fox'.

Why We Have Surnames

Eighty thousand (80,000) years ago, while our early human ancestors still all lived in Africa, there were only a few hundred of us altogether. It would have been possible for you to meet every human being alive. If our ancestors used names at all (we don't know if they did) they

Find out more

Two excellent Internet sites for learning about surnames are:

http://www.nationaltrustnames.org.uk/
This site creates maps showing where people with your surname live now, and where they were back in 1881.

http://www.taliesin-arlein.net/names/search.php
This site will tell you how many people share your surname in England and Wales today, and how popular your surname is.

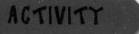

ACTIVITY

Play Chinese whispers

Many surnames have changed due to people not hearing what was being said very clearly. The Scottish surname Galbraith, for example, was recorded as Coldbreath in Sussex. To find out how this can happen, try playing Chinese Whispers.

1 Sit in a circle with your friends.

2 Whisper a surname into the ear of the person sitting to your right.

3 That person must then whisper the same surname into the ear of the person sitting to their right.

4 This continues round the circle until the surname is whispered back to you.

5 Everyone has whispered what they think they heard, but often you'll find that they have not heard what the surname actually was. What is whispered to you may be completely different to the surname with which you began.

Did you know?

Coldbreath is what people in Sussex thought Scottish immigrants called Galbraith said when they introduced themselves.

would probably have had just one. But later, much later, when the world became crowded, there simply were not enough first names to go around.

'Hello Mary! How's Mary?'

'Mary's fine, thanks. I saw her and Mary yesterday. They told me Mary was ill.'

'Mary's ill! How terrible. Has Mary been to see her?'

It makes no sense, does it? They can't possibly know which Marys they are talking about. Actually, you've probably experienced this problem yourself at school, whenever there is more than person in the class with the same name. You have probably used nicknames to tell such people apart.

Nicknames

A nickname is a second name made up for people by their friends. Nicknames often have something to do with the way people behave or look. When I was 18, my circle of friends included a confusing number of Marks, and I remember there being Short Mark, Tall Mark, and Mad Mark.

This is actually how surnames came into being. About 1,000 years ago, at the start of the Middle Ages, most people had nicknames like this. In those days the nickname came after the first name – Mark the Short, Mark the Mad and so on. During the next couple of hundred years something rather odd happened. Instead of each person having a nickname that suited them, people started to use the same nicknames as their fathers.

We don't know exactly why this happened, but it was probably because lords and tax collectors wanted to be able to identify the same family over a long period of time. They forced families to keep the same nickname, and the nicknames became surnames. These surnames are sometimes termed 'hereditary surnames', because 'hereditary' is a term for something that passes down in a family.

This process happened all over the British Isles, first in Ireland and England and later in Scotland and Wales.

Did you know?

In Wales, some families only started using hereditary surnames in the 1800s, less than 200 years ago. Because many men in Wales at the time were called David, Thomas, William, Evan and John, very common Welsh surnames include Davis, Thomas, Williams, Evans and Jones. These mean 'son of David', 'son of Thomas', 'son of William', 'son of Evan' and 'son of John' respectively.

How to decode a surname

Surnames started passing down in families during the Middle Ages. A lot of them use Medieval terms, or reflect Medieval names that were popular at the time. They are like time-capsules, because they have remained unchanged for hundreds of years. They are fascinating because they tell you something about the ancestor who had the nickname that became the surname in the first place.

The types of nicknames that became surnames fall into five groups. Most surnames, wherever they are from in the world, will fall into one of the same five groups.

Very few people are Archers by profession today although it was a common trade in the Middle Ages.

Nicknames

The first type of surname started with the way someone behaved, or how they looked. The surname Short indicates that the family's ancestor was not very tall. The surname White means the ancestor was very pale, or had white hair. Armstrong means the ancestor had strong arms. Some common names are nicknames written in other languages. In Scotland and Ireland, for example, people spoke Gaelic. The Scottish surname Cameron, for example, is Gaelic for 'hooked nose'. The technical term for this type of surname is *sobriquet*, meaning 'nickname'.

Parents' names

The second type of surname is from parents' names. They often end 'son' or 's'. Richardson and Richards both mean 'son of Richard'. Johnson and Jones both mean 'son of John'. In Gaelic-speaking Scotland and Ireland, Mac (or Mc) meant 'son'. MacDonald means 'son of Donald' and McGregor 'son of Gregor'. The Irish also use 'O' to mean 'descendant of'. O'Kelly means 'descendant of Kelly' and O'Donovan 'descendant of Donovan'. Some people were named after their mother instead. The surname Orange means 'son of Orangia', a girls' name used about 800 years ago, that went out of fashion. The technical term for this type of surname is *patronymic*, which is Latin for 'father's name', or *matronymic*, meaning mother's name.

Place names

Thirdly, surnames can come from place names. Families who owned places might use the place names as their surnames. The Birmingham family owned Birmingham, and the Berkeleys (also spelled Barclay) own Berkeley Castle in Gloucestershire. Families who didn't own any land might be known by the name of the place where they lived. The Lincoln family gained their surname because their ancestors were from Lincoln, and the London family were from London. The technical term for this type of surname is *locative* - where the family was located.

Types of place

Fourthly, surnames can come from descriptions of where ancestors lived. People who lived by a wood, hill, forest or lake might be surnamed Woods, Hill, Forest or Lake. People who lived by man-made things like a bridge, castle, hall (a type of big house) or church might be surnamed Bridge, Castle, Hall or Church. The technical term for this type of surname is *topographic* – describing the family by the place where they lived.

A medieval farmer's children may have been given the surname Farmer.

Jobs

Finally, people's jobs could could become surnames. A farmer or painter might be surnamed Farmer or Painter. Many of the jobs people did in the Middle Ages are no longer very common today, but they are remembered by surnames. Men who fired bows and arrows were archers, hence the surname Archer. The fletcher was the man who made the arrows, hence the surname Fletcher. The bowyer made bows, hence the surname Bowyer. The surname Carrot means someone who grew carrots. The technical term for this type of surname is *metonymic*, which actually means 'alternative name', but is used for surnames derived from jobs.

How surnames pass down in families: Down the father's line

Until around the 1970s, when couples married, the woman always started using her husband's surname. Their children were all given the father's surname. A daughter in the family would use her father's surname until she married, when she would take her husband's. A son in the family would use his father's surname all his life, and pass it on in turn to his children. In this way, surnames passed down the family tree along the men's lines, passing from father to son, generation after generation. That is why you are probably using the same surname as your father, and his father, and his father, and so on.

Down the mother's line

There are exceptions to this rule. Children who are adopted are given the surname of the parents who adopted them, and may not know the surname of their original parents. In the past, when couples who were not married had children, the children were given the surname of the mother, not the father. If your great grandparents were not married, then you may find that your surname comes from your father's father's mother's line. Nowadays, many couples have children without first getting married. The children might be given either the mother's or the father's surnames, or both. Each family is different: that's part of the fun, though it may make life more difficult for genealogists in the future.

Double-barrelled surnames

When one surname was not enough, people sometimes used two. These are called double-barrelled surnames, or hyphenated surnames, because they are usually attached by a hyphen, like this: '-'. Usually, the surnames will both come from the family's ancestors. A family called Lloyd-Roberts is probably descended from a Mr Lloyd, who married a Miss Roberts. These surnames are handy for genealogists, because they tell you about not one but two lines of ancestors.

Spelling surnames

The same surname can be spelled in several different ways. This is because in the past very few people could read or write, so they did not know how to spell their surnames. When other people (such as priests, or clerks) wrote the surnames down, there was no point asking 'how do you spell that?' because nobody knew. So the surname Carrott could be written down Carrott, or Carrot, or Carott, Carritt or Carrartt, or even Karrott – they all sound the same. Do not be surprised to find the surnames in your family being spelled in all sorts of different ways.

The surname Croker comes from someone who made crockery

Now, what eats carrots? Believe it or not, there is a real surname, Rabbit. Recently I came across a lady whose parents gave her the first name 'Queen'. She married a Mr Rabbit, so her name became Queen Rabbit (I really haven't made that up). The surname Rabbit has nothing to do with fluffy animals, though: it just sounds the same. It is actually a slightly altered version of the name Robert. If you say 'Robert' and 'Rabbit' over and over again very quickly, you can see how, over hundreds of years, they can become confused. The surname Rabbit means simply 'son of Robert'.

There are plenty of surnames that sound like one thing but mean another:

Croker is not a name for a loud frog, but a metonymic surname for someone who made pots and plates, that we still sometimes call 'crockery'.

Gibbons. We are distantly related to monkeys and gibbons, but that's not what this surname means. In the Middle Ages, 'Gib' was short for 'Gilbert', and this is in fact a patronymic surname meaning 'son of Gilbert'.

Leek is a Viking name for a stream

Leek is not a name for someone who looked like a vegetable, as you might suppose, but a locative surname meaning someone from a place called Leek in Staffordshire. The place name is a Viking one meaning 'stream'.

Parker. Not a nosey-parker, but someone who looked after parks, back in the days where parks were large enclosed areas where noblemen kept stags to be hunted.

Raddish is a locative surname meaning someone from Redditch, Worcestershire. The place name means 'a ditch where reeds grew'.

Salmon sounds a bit fishy, doesn't it? It's actually a shortened version of the name Salamon or Solomon, and is a patronymic meaning 'son of Solomon'.

Slaughter sounds nasty, but is a locative surname for someone from the village of Slaughter in Herefordshire. The place name was spelled Sclostre a thousand years ago, and was Anglo-Saxon for a 'muddy place'.

Crows and Moles

The 1861 census for Milton Ernest, Bedfordshire, shows a family of Crows and Moles living next door to each other. Do you think they quarrelled? The surname Crow was a nickname for people whose hair was black as a crow's. The surname Mole was a nickname too, but for someone very small, from the Viking word *moli*, meaning 'a crumb'.

Same surname, wrong family? Smith and Jones

Many surnames started in one place, with one person. Everyone with the surname is therefore related, somehow. But there are plenty of surnames that don't just belong to one family. This applies especially to very common ones, like Smith and Jones.

Smith means 'a smith' – the man who used to put iron horseshoes on horses. Each village had a smith, so lots of smiths, who were not related to each other, took the surname Smith.

Equally, Jones is Welsh for 'son of John'. Many Welshmen were called John, but were not related to each other. Many

The 'St Columba' pedigree

Family trees or pedigrees are special when they cross continents, and cultures, and social classes. St Columba (who died in 597 AD) was descended from King Niall of the Nine Hostages, High Kings of Ireland. Although he was a prince, Columba became a monk and went to Scotland to convert the pagans there. He founded the monastery of Iona, on the west coast of Scotland.

St Columba's brothers' descendants became abbots of Dunkeld near Perth. One of these abbots married the daughter of King Malcolm II of Scotland, and their sons were King Duncan I and Maldred of Northumberland.

Not long afterwards, surnames started coming into use. Various different descendants of Maldred took on different surnames, depending on where they were at the time. Amazingly they are all descended through St Columba's family, from the High Kings of Ireland:

George Washington was the first President of the United States of America

1. The Nevilles

One line married the heiress or daughter of the great Neville family, and adopted the surname Neville themselves. The Neville descendants of St Columba's family included Richard Neville, 16th Earl of Warwick (d. 1471), nicknamed 'Warwick the Kingmaker' because he was powerful enough to decide who sat on the English throne.

2. The Hansards

Another line were nicknamed 'Hansard'. Hansard is an old name for a cutlass or sword – they were a warlike family. A further line became Earls of Dunbar, and took the surname Dunbar. Other lines took the surnames Kestern, Edlingham, Letham and Strickland.

3. The Washingtons

Yet another line settled at Washington in County Durham, and became the Washington family. Their descendants include George Washington (d. 1799) first President of the United States, after whom the American capital Washington DC is named. It's extraordinary that the first occupant of the White House can be traced right back to the High Kings of Ireland.

of their sons became surnamed Jones, so there are many Joneses who are not related in the slightest.

Sometimes, when researching a family tree, you may come across a record, or a family tree, showing people with the surname you are researching. You should make a note of what you find. But don't just decide that, because they have the right surname, they must be your ancestors.

Famous surnames

Everest

Many people share their surname with a famous person, or with something named after a famous person. The tallest mountain in the world is Mount Everest, in the Himalayas. It was named after Sir George Everest (1790-1866), who was in charge of making maps of India, Tibet and Nepal, on whose border the great mountain stands. 'Everest' is an example of a surname that has changed over the centuries. Originally, it was Evereux (pronounced Ever-oh!), a place in Normandy, France. People from Evereux took the name as their surname and then settled in England, where it changed to Everest. By a series of chance happenings, therefore, a French place name ended up becoming the name of the tallest mountain on Earth.

Frisbie

Joseph P. Frisbie (d. 1940) had a factory making fruit pies in Bridgeport, Connecticut, U.S.A. His family surname also came from a place name – Frisby, Lincolnshire. Joseph's pies were packaged in circular tins. His employees used to relax at lunchtime by throwing the lids of these tins to each other, and trying to catch them. From this game developed the plastic disk that people play with in parks and on beaches – frisbees.

Defoe

Streets are often named after people. Sometimes, the town council will name a street after a famous person who lived there. Defoe Road, in Stoke Newington, London is named after Daniel Defoe (1661-1731). Defoe lived there when his book *Robinson Crusoe* was published in 1719. The surname Defoe used to be De Foe, originally spelled De Vaux. It is the surname of a family who came from a place called Vaux in France.

Jermyn

Sometimes, people named streets after themselves. In London's West End is Jermyn Street, famed for its shops selling shirts. It was built by Henry Jermyn, Earl of St Albans (1605-84), who also built nearby St Albans Street. His surname comes from an ancestor's name, and means 'son of Jermyn or Germain'.

Edible surnames

Many types of food are named after their makers. Kellogg's, who make breakfast cereals, was founded as the Battle Creek Toasted Corn Flake Company in Michigan, USA, in 1906 by Will Keith Kellogg (1860-1951). The firm was renamed Kellogg's in 1922. Cadbury's chocolate has been made by the Cadbury family since 1824, when the firm was founded in Birmingham by John Cadbury (1801-1889). Heinz foods grew from the family firm of Henry John Heinz, founded in 1869 in Pennsylvania, USA, originally making tomato ketchup and then branching out to produce tinned food like baked beans as well.

What do you think these names mean? Kellogg is a good example of a surname changing gradually over the centuries. In the Middle Ages it was a surname taken from an ancestor's job –'kill hog'. A hog was a pig, so the original Mr 'Killhog' was a pork butcher. Cadbury is a surname from a place name – John Cadbury's ancestors came from a place called Cadbury. In Old English, 'bury' meant 'a fort', so Cadbury was a fort belonging to someone called Cada. Heinz is a German form of the surname Henry, meaning 'son of Henry'.

Daniel Defoe has a street in London named after him. You'll find that many streets in London are named after famous historical figures.

Edible surnames: The Heinz family are well-known for their baked beans

Too many Henrys

Some families have their own customs, that can become rather confusing. The Princes of Reuss in Germany decided to call all the boys born in their family Henry, in honour of a German Emperor, Henry VI (Henry the sixth). To tell the boys apart, each had to be given a number, in Roman numerals. The first Henry was Henry I (the first), who died in 1162. He had three sons, each called Henry – Henry II (the second), Henry III (the third) and Henry IV (the fourth). They called all their sons Henry, continuing the numbering system. After a few generations, as you can imagine, there were quite a lot of Henrys around. The family divided into several branches, each still calling all their sons Henry. By the 1800s, one branch had got up to Henry LXXIV (Henry the seventy-fourth)!

What names mean

Most personal names have meanings. George is Greek for 'farmer' and Phoebe is Greek for 'bright'. Rachel is Jewish for 'ewe' (a female sheep) and Nathan is Jewish for 'given by God'. Mira is Hindi for 'ocean' and Sanjeev is Hindi for 'full of life'.

First Names

First names are also called personal names, or forenames. In Christian families they are called Christian names, because they are given to children when they are christened.

As you explore back up your family tree, you will probably find that more than one person in the family had the same personal name. Sometimes this is a coincidence. But most of the time it is deliberate. Parents often used to name their children after themselves, their own parents or their brothers and sisters. People say such names are 'family names', and deliberately pass them on to their own children. They remind us of ancestors who had the same personal name, who may have lived long ago.

Naming patterns

Some cultures have strict rules governing the naming of children. In Greek families, the eldest son is almost always named after his father's father. In Scotland, you will often find that the eldest son and daughter are named after the father's parents, and the second eldest son and daughter after the mother's parents. You can sometimes guess what the earlier generation were probably called, just from the names given to their grandchildren.

Middle names

When people have personal names and surnames that are both quite common, it can be difficult to tell them apart. Being called John Smith or Ann Taylor means that you can be confused easily with thousands of people with the same two names. Believe it or not, there are even a few people around with my unusual name, Anthony Adolph. Since the late 1700s, therefore, many children have been given an extra name as a middle name: I was christened Anthony Richard Adolph, for example.

Fathers' names

In southern India, people usually have three names: first the name of their village, then the name of their father, and then a personal name. The Romans also used three names: first the personal name, then the surname, then a nickname. In Greece, people usually have two names, their personal name and surname, but often include a middle name which is the name of their father. If a Greek is called Nicholas Georgios Valinakis, you can be sure his father was called Georgios Valinakis.

Chinese middle names

In China, the middle name is a 'generation name'. Each family has a special poem, some of which were given to the family by a Chinese Emperor. The first generation of the family uses the first word of the poem as their middle name. Everyone in the second generation of the family uses the second word of the poem as their middle name. Each person in the third generation of the same family uses the poem's third word, and so on. When two Chinese people of the same surname meet, they can compare their generation names. If their generation names come from the same poem, they know they belong to the same family. If their generation names are the same, then they know they belong to the same generation of the same family.

12

Things That We Inherit

You will almost certainly have inherited your surname from either your father or mother. But that's just the start of things you might have inherited, from the colour of your hair, to your blood group or even a title. There may even be things that you could inherit, that you don't know about yet, and that you may find when you explore your family tree further back.

Inheritance

When things pass down from parents to their children, the process is called 'inheriting'. People inherit money, houses and objects from their parents or grandparents when they die. We say that these are 'passed down in the family', and call them 'heirlooms'. We sometimes take old objects for granted, and don't realise that they may have been passed down in the family, perhaps for many generations.

I used to think that an heirloom meant a weaving loom, on which people made things out of human hair. I was wrong, and in any case 'heir' is spelled differently to 'hair'. An 'heir' is a person who inherits things from someone who has died. In the old days, an 'heirloom' was a tool or piece of useful machinery, like a weaving loom, that was passed on from parents to their children. Now the word is used for any object that is passed on or inherited in that way.

Sometimes, people leave things to other relatives, or friends, or charities. Some old ladies leave their money to their cats. You could say that these lucky mewers are hairy heirs! Receiving these things (whether you are a human or a cat) is called inheritance.

Surnames are inherited. You have almost certainly inherited yours from one of your parents. Old family papers can be inherited. So too can things like how you speak and what religion you practise.

How we speak

Parents pass all sorts of other things on to their children. Most children who speak English learned to speak simply by listening to their parents talking. If your parents lived in Spain and spoke only Spanish, you would not be able to understand what I have just written. Your family use certain expressions, and you can't help but pick these up and use them yourself. When my mother's father was surprised, he used to say 'lummy!', and so do I. I have inherited this expression from him. If your family comes from overseas, they might still speak their ancestors' language. They may have taught you to speak it too, or if not they might still use some words in that language, that you use too. You will have inherited the practise of using these words.

Superstitions

For luck, I say 'touch wood', and make sure I touch something that is wooden. This is because my mother says and does the same thing. My mother was taught to say this by her father. Who knows how many generations of my ancestors have taught their children the same thing? Ten? Fifty? Maybe as far back as the ancient Britons, who thought some trees, like oaks, yews and ashes, were sacred, so they probably did touch them for luck.

In Scotland, some people say 'hairy wood's the best' and tap their heads for luck. It is a joke, saying that your head is made of wood. But it is another version of the same superstition, and again may have been passed down through countless generations of Scots.

Many people have the superstition that bad luck will befall them if the 13th day of the month is a Friday. Luckily, this doesn't happen very often. The correct term for this fear is paraskavedekatriaphobia!

Why you look like you do

In Chapter 5 I showed you how to make a family tree including your ancestors' faces, so that you could see whether or not you looked like any of them.

We all inherit the way we look from our parents. You often hear people talking about new-born babies and saying 'she looks just like her mother!' or something similar. Now, you might look very similar to one of your parents, but it's impossible to look exactly the same. This is because they way you look comes from both your father and your mother.

If a black cat walks in front of you, you will have bad luck. That was a superstition held by the ancient Sumerians (see page 94) and it has been passed down in many families to the present day. However some families in Britain believe exactly the opposite!

Our genes

Our bodies are made of millions of tiny cells. Each one contains genes, that tell the cells what to do. These genes govern everything about you. There are genes to say what colour hair you will have; what colour eyes; how tall you will be; what skin colour you will have and so on.

We all inherit the genes that decide the way we look from both parents. But which genes a baby will receive from either parent is a random process, like a lottery. In each human being, the amount of genes that come from the mother as opposed to from the father is different. If this were not so, then brothers and sisters in the same family would look absolutely identical. Twins are identical, because they received their genes from their parents at exactly the same time. But in all other cases, brothers and sisters will look slightly different to each other, or sometimes completely different. One brother might be taller than another. He will have inherited a gene from one of his parents that makes him tall, whilst the other might have inherited a gene from the other parent that makes him short.

Whatever genes you have, however, you know that they all come from your parents, who in turn inherited their appearance from their parents, and so on right back up the family tree. You can have fun working out which genes come from your mother and which come from your father, and in turn which of your grandparents had passed them on down the line.

Find out more

Ask your mother if she uses any recipes for cakes, pies, jams and so on, that were given to her by her mother. If Granny is still alive, ask if any of these came from her mother in turn. Just think how many generations of your family might have eaten food made using exactly the same old recipe. Learn to follow the same recipes to carry on your tasty family traditions.

Identical twins look the same because they have exactly the same genes.

Body quirks

Here are some examples (out of thousands) of things you can inherit through your genes. The numbered illustrations on the opposite page show some examples. **(1)** Whether or not you can bend your thumb back like this is decided by your genes. If you can bend your thumb back, can one of your parents? Can one of their parents? If so, which other relatives on that side of the family can do it? If you can't do it, which of your parents can't? Maybe both. **(2)** The same applies to being able to roll your tongue. **(3)** Can you make the Vulcan hand sign that Mr Spock uses in the TV series *Star Trek*? Some people can do these things completely naturally, and others simply cannot, no matter how hard they try.

Your face has lots of different parts that come from different genes. **(4)** Ear lobes are a good example. Are yours attached to the side of your head, or does the bottom bit dangle down? A gene has decided which. Usually, your mother or father (or both) will have the same sort of ear lobes as you. Say you have dangly earlobes. If you have only one parent with the same lobes, then you have probably inherited this part of your ear from them. Now, how about their parents? Can you tell which grandparent has passed down that particular gene? **(5)** Look at the shape of your lips, especially the bit in the middle of the top of your upper lip. Some people's go straight across, and others have a very prominent dip in the middle.

You can also look at the colouring of your eyes, hair and skin and the shape of:

• Your nose seen from the side
• Your nose seen from the front, especially your nostrils
• Your eyebrows and the ability to move them
• Your chin
• Your cheek bones: some are just below the eyes, and really stand out, and others you hardly notice

How Genes work

By the way, don't worry if you can do something neither of your parents can. It doesn't mean you are adopted. Sometimes you can have a gene that lets you do something, but another one that stops you. For example, if your mother has both such genes that relate to thumb bending, she may not able to bend her thumb backwards. But she may only have passed on to you the gene that lets you bend back your thumb, so you can do it but she can't.

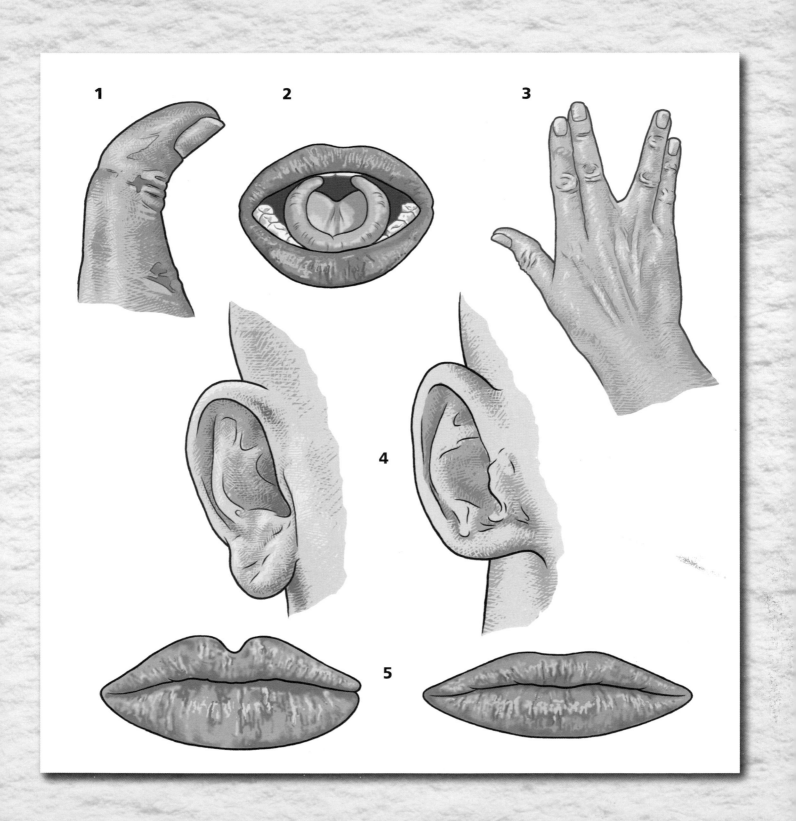

Collecting heirlooms

1 See if you can find objects that were owned by as many of your grandparents and great grandparents as possible. These might be an old photograph, or an object that they owned, such as a book or a medal. One of the old saucepans in the kitchen might have been used by your great grandmother to cook meals during the Second World War. That old walking stick in the hallway might have been leaned on by your great-great-great grandfather during the reign of Edward VII.

2 Ask any old relatives if they have any heirlooms or inherited objects and whether you can look after them.

3 Keep the heirlooms in your Family History Box, or if there is not room, make a special box for heirlooms.

4 See if you can collect one object (or drawing of an object) for each of your grandparents and great grandparents. Don't worry if you cannot, because lots of things get thrown away, but the more you can collect the better. You may find heirlooms that have been in the family so long that nobody knows who owned them originally. As you explore your family tree, you may be able to discover more about them and where they came from.

TIP

Your family might be kind enough to give you some old objects – little things that your grandparents, great grandparents and perhaps even earlier ancestors owned. However, they might be fond of them, and want to keep these objects themselves. In that case, take a fresh piece of paper, and draw the object – the walking stick, or whatever it happens to be. Write down what the object is, who told you about it, and who owned it originally.

Some of my family heirlooms

1 Teddy is from my mother's family.

2 My mother's mother once wore the star-shaped decoration, which was given to the wives of officers in her husband's Second World War regiment.

3 The clock, in its travelling case, belonged to mother's Uncle Willie.

4 The book was also Uncle Willie's. He wrote his name in Latin in 1921.

5 This knife was my father's sister's, and has her initials, 'R.A.' scratched on the handle.

6 My father's mother owned the sherry glass, and won the two medals immediately to the left for ballroom dancing in the 1960s.

7 The buttons come from uniforms worn by my father's father, who was in the Palestinian Police.

8 The spoon standing up was my father's father's christening spoon, with his initials, 'J.A.', from 1910.

9 My father's father's mother owned the sugar-tongs, which are resting against Teddy's leg.

Clans and Tartans

In Scotland and Ireland, many ancestors belonged to clans. A clan was rather like a big family, that controlled an area of land. There would be a clan chief, who was chosen from amongst the family of the previous chief. He would not necessarily be his eldest son: he might be a nephew, or even a cousin, chosen for his ability to lead the clan in war. Therefore, most clan members were descended from an earlier clan chief, one way or another.

The men of the clan would farm the clan's lands, and also join the clan's army in times of war. Clans tended to be at war most of the time, usually because they spent a lot of time stealing each other's cattle, or seeking revenge for relatives killed in earlier raids.

The clans have stopped fighting each other, but their descendants are still very proud of their clan membership. The clans still elect chiefs and hold clan gatherings, usually in their ancestral homes. Many descendants of the clans, who live all over the world, from Canada to New Zealand, fly back occasionally to Ireland or Scotland, to celebrate their family origins.

These are examples of some of the different tartans that Scottish families inherit. They often use their tartans to make kilts, like those on the right.

Tartans

Many Scottish clans have a distinctive tartan. This is a type of woollen cloth, woven with a pattern of criss-crossing lines. Originally, each village had its own pattern, taught by mothers to their daughters, and passed down over hundreds of years. In old Scotland, if you met a complete stranger but recognised the pattern of their tartan, you could tell from whence he came.

Bonnie Prince Charlie's rebellion against George II in 1745-1746 included many fierce Scotsmen, all wearing their local tartans. When the English crushed the rebellion, they forbade the Scots to wear tartan any more. This made tartan into a symbol of freedom, and of Scottish families' pride in their origins. After the ban was lifted in 1782, most Scottish families and clans adopted a distinctive tartan of their own. People who are Scottish, or have a Scottish ancestors, still enjoy wearing tartan on special days, like weddings.

Women wear skirts or dresses made with their family tartan, and men wear kilts. Kilts are like skirts, worn with a sporran (a leather or fur purse that hangs off the belt) and a *sgian dubh* (a Gaelic word pronounced 'skee-an-doo') a short knife that Scotsmen keep sticking out of the top of one of their socks. You might think the idea of a man wearing a skirt is amusing, but it's best to treat Scotsmen wearing kilts with great respect. The kilt is a symbol of family honour, and Scotsmen don't take kindly to people sniggering at them.

These two boys, Fred and Ernest, are wearing kilts, and the boy on the left has a sporran dangling from his belt too. Old photographs of Scottish ancestors sometimes show them wearing their father's clan tartan or the clan tartan of one of their mother's or grandmother's ancestors.

Plant emblems

Scottish Highlanders also showed to which clan they belonged by sticking a sprig of a particular plant in their hats. For example, if you saw someone wearing a sprig of seaweed in their hat, you'd know he was a MacNeil. The Frasers had sprigs of yew in their hats, the MacLeans wore sprigs of holly and the MacLeods used juniper. Each badge has a story attached to it. The Morrisons' badge of driftweed (a type of seaweed) recalls the story of their founder, an Irish lord called Ghille Mhuire. He was shipwrecked, but clung to a piece of driftwood, and was washed safely ashore in the Hebrides, which are islands off the north-west coast of Scotland.

Driftweed is the emblem for the Morrison Clan. Holly is the emblem for the MacLeans. The Fraser clan used to wear sprigs of yew in their hats.

Tales of the MacLeods

Each clan has wonderful stories about its founders, and their brave deeds. The MacLeods of the island of Skye (part of the Hebrides) claim descent from Leod, a Viking chieftan. He founded Dunvegan Castle, where his descendant, Hugh, the 30th Clan Chief, still lives.

In the castle you can see the Fairy Flag, a piece of cloth so ancient that is half falling to pieces. Tradition holds that,

hundreds of years ago, a chief of the clan married a beautiful Fairy princess and had a son. Her father the Fairy King would only allow her to stay with her husband for a year. When she was forced to leave her husband, she made him promise never to let their son cry, for she could not bear to hear him being unhappy. The chief kept his word, but once, during a great feast, the child's nanny crept away to watch the chief dancing, and the child started to cry. The Fairy princess at once appeared, and wrapped her son in a piece of Fairy-woven cloth which, as I am sure you know, has magical properties.

The Fairies told the chief that if he or his descendants waved the Fairy Flag, they would come to his help three times. Once, a chief waved it because the MacDonalds were besieging Dunvegan. The Fairies came and drove the enemies away. Another time, all the MacLeods' cows were

Dunvegan Castle, an ancestral seat of the MacLeods of Skye, and home of the Fairy Flag.

dying of plague, so the chief waved the flag and the Fairies magically cured the animals. The flag has yet to be waved for the third and last time. During the Second World War, when everyone thought the German army was going to invade Britain, the Chief of the Clan MacLeod was ready to take the Fairy Flag to the White Cliffs of Dover to wave it, so that the Fairy King and his shining army would come and save Britain. Luckily, Hitler's Germans never invaded, and the third and last wave of the flag remains in reserve.

Clan societies

If you have Scottish or Irish ancestors, you might find that they belonged to a clan. Many have Clan Societies and websites. You can use these to find out if your ancestors had a special tartan or a plant badge. There are books on clans and tartans in most libraries. A good one for Scotland is Roddy Martine's *Scottish Clan and Family Names: their arms, origins and tartans* (Mainstream Publishing, 1987, 1992).

TITLES

Duke – from the Roman *dux*, used for a military leader.

Marquis – originally a French title for the military commanders of 'marks', which were lawless regions bordering other countries.

Earl – from the Saxon *eorl*, for the commander of a county and its soldiers.

Viscount – the French equivalent of 'Earl' was 'Count'. A 'vice count' was therefore someone who stood in for an earl.

Baron – a word that meant 'warrior' in Roman times, and was used later for someone who held a large area of land in return for fighting for the king.

Titles

Some families are lucky enough to have titles that pass down in families, from fathers to their eldest sons. The grandest titles are those of royalty – Emperors (or Empresses) and Kings (or Queens). There used to be quite a few Emperors (in Germany, Austria and Ethiopia, for example) but now there is just one, the Emperor of Japan. There are plenty more kings and queens, including the head of our own Royal Family.

Monarchs like Kings and Queens can give noble titles to other families. Many countries, all over the world, have families of lords, with titles. In Britain, the lordly titles are Duke, Marquis, Earl, Viscount and Baron. In this list, Dukes are the most important, and Barons the least important. There are also Baronets, who are not actually noble, but inherit the title 'Sir' (you sometimes see 'baronet' shortened to 'bt'). Nowadays, a lot of the titles given to people are called 'life peerages' – they are for the person to whom it is given, but cannot be passed down to their eldest son. But in the old days, titles like this were almost always hereditary – they passed down from the father to his oldest son, generation after generation, as long as there were sons to inherit it.

Find out more

Irish Clan Societies are listed at **www.celts.org/clans/**, and Scottish ones at **www.electricscotland.com/ webclans/clanmenu.htm.**

Lordly ancestors

Very few people have titles. But, in a lot of family trees – perhaps even yours – if you go back far enough, you might find a family with a title. Some people can be a bit snobby about titles. If they have an ancestor who was a duke, they think they are better than everyone else. That's not necessarily true, but it does mean you can find more about your family tree. Families with titles tend to have had books written about them, and their family trees are often quite easy to find. Many are on the Internet, and also in books in libraries, especially *Burke's Peerage*. This is an enormous book that records all the family trees of people with titles. There are other books published by Burkes too, such as *Burke's Landed Gentry*. This records families who had no titles, but who owned a lot of land, so were very grand anyway.

Prince Edward, the Queen's third son, was made Earl of Wessex when he got married in 1999.

Coats of Arms

Coats of arms are painted shields, that are inherited in families. You often see coats of arms when you visit castles. This is because in the Middle Ages, knights rode into battle covered in shining armour, with helmets that covered up

their faces. Nobody could tell who was who, so each knight would have a brightly painted design on his shield. You would recognise the coats of arms of the knights on your own side, and be careful to avoid killing them.

Coats of arms are inherited by all the children in the family, but only the sons pass them on to their own children. This way, they usually stay with the same surname. Some coats of arms started being used 800 years ago, and are still being used by the same family today. As we don't wear armour now, coats of arms are usually shown on flags, writing paper, rings and suchlike.

Heraldry

Exploring coats of arms is called heraldry. It is a complicated subject, because its rules have developed gradually over the last 800 years, but it's good fun too. The people who make sure the right people are using the right coats of arms are called heralds, and they work for the Queen. The English heralds live at The College of Arms in London, near St Paul's Cathedral. They still use old-fashioned-sounding titles that make people smile when they hear them for the first time. The chief herald is called Garter King of Arms, and other heralds have names like Richmond Herald, and Bluemantle Pursuivant of Arms. In Scotland, the chief herald is called Lord Lyon King of Arms, and the chief herald in the Republic of Ireland is called (less excitingly) the Chief Herald of Ireland.

Who had coats of arms?

Coats of arms tended to be granted or given to families who had titles, or who owned a lot of land, or just had a lot of money. A family might lose all its money, but you cannot lose the right to use the family coat of arms. Consequently, there are quite a lot of poor families now who can use coats of arms because their ancestors had one.

Mottos, crests and shields

Coats of arms are painted on shields, or shield-shaped pieces of paper. Sometimes, these shields are surrounded by other things.

There may be a scroll, showing the family motto. This may be written in Latin or English (or some other language). It will usually be a stirring phrase, like 'Brave and True', or 'In God we Trust'. Mottos are never the opposite, like 'Give up and go Home'.

Above the shield, you might find a helmet and a crest. The crest sits on the helmet, or perches on the shield itself. The crest sometime shows an object or creature that also appears on the coat of arms. They date back to the days of Medieval battles, when the crest was made of painted leather and sat on top of the knight's helmet for extra identification. There is often some frilly cloth draped over the helmet. When a knight wore his metal helmet in the summer, the sun could make it unbearably terribly hot, so he would put a piece of cloth over the top, to try to shade it a bit.

Finally, very grand families, usually those who had titles, or who were kings or queens, had supporters. These are animals (or people) who are painted on either side of the shield, holding it up.

The coat of arms of the MacLeods, painted by heraldic artist Tom Meek. As this is Scottish the motto is over the crest. English mottos usually go under the shield.

Animals in arms

The creatures and objects shown on coats of arms are often relevant to the family's history. Some truly ancient arms depict animals that were probably originally tribal emblems. In Ireland, the MacDermots and their descendants the Crowleys have a wild boar in their arms. The boar was probably an ancient tribal symbol, respected in much the same way as Native American Indians revere the animals they carve on their totem poles.

Design your own coat of arms

Official coats of arms have to be granted by the Heralds, on behalf of the King or Queen. But there's no harm in you making one up just for yourself, and it's rather fun to do.

1 Choose which helm you like best and trace it. Then, move the tracing of the helm under the mantling. Trace the mantling around the helm.

2 Move the tracing down, choose a shield that you like and trace it under the helm.

3 Chose a ribbon for your motto and trace it under the shield.

4 Chose whatever bright colours you like, and put as little or as much on the shield as you want (but not too much, or it will look crowded. Remember, if you ever use your coat of arms in a battle, you will want to be easily spotted by your friends).

5 You can decide on whatever motto you want, but make it appropriate to you. Some mottos are clever puns on the family name. The Neville family's motto is 'wish for nothing vile (or unpleasant)', but they display it in Latin, *Ne vile veils*, the start of which almost spells out the name 'Neville'. The motto of the Marquisses of Ailesbury was 'Think and Thank', which is a good motto for anyone.

This example shows you how to assemble your chosen helm, shield and ribbon with the mantling.

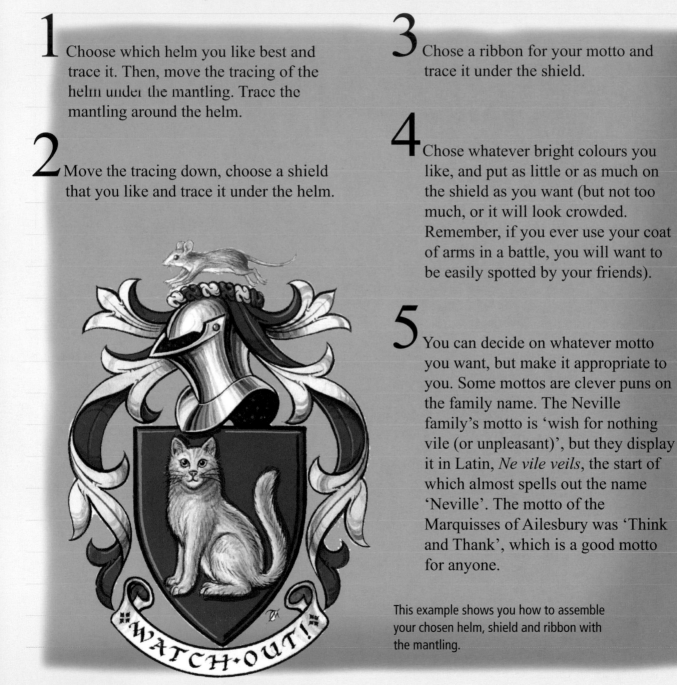

1.

2.

3.

13

Using And Understanding Old Records

Research is like a treasure hunt. It is fun because you keep finding clues to the answer. These clues can include old family papers. Other members of the family may already have started tracing the family tree, so they may have found original records in archives. By using records, you can start tracing the family tree back far beyond the limits of your oldest relatives' memories.

Written records

Ever since humans invented writing, people have been recording who their ancestors were. Darius I of Persia (who died in 486 BC) left a famous inscription that can still be seen carved in huge letters on a rock in Iran, proclaiming:

> I am Darius the Great King, King of Kings, King in Persia…
> my father was Hystaspes; Hystaspes' father was Arsames; Arsames' father was Ariaramnes; Ariaramnes' father was Teispes; Teispes' father was Achaemenes… For this reason we are called Achaemenians. From long ago we have been noble.

In Britain, we have records carved in rock too. The Pillar of Eliseg near Valle Crucis Abbey, Denbighshire, Wales, was put up by Concenn, King of Powys, who died in AD 855, and proclaims him as

The Pillar of Eliseg: an ancient record of British family history.

> Concenn son of Cattell, Cattell son of Brohcmail,
> Brohcmail son of Eliseg, Eliseg son of Guoillauc…
> [descended from] Maximus, the king, who killed the king of the Romans.

This was an impressive claim, and an exciting piece of family tree for anyone descended from King Concenn. And a surprising number of people with Welsh ancestry actually are his descendants.

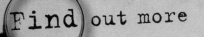

Find out more

Where are your family papers?
Family papers and Bibles are usually kept by the oldest daughter of the family. Your father's father's family papers, therefore, are most likely to be with your father's father's sister (your great aunt) or, if she has died, with her daughter.

Later stone inscriptions take the form of gravestones, which you will see in churchyards, and 'memorial inscriptions', that are usually inside churches. Most date from the 1700s onwards. These usually give family tree details, perhaps naming husband and wife, with dates of death, ages and sometimes even children.

In Memory Of
Malcolm MacDonald Rodel 1785 - 1873
His wife
Margaret Mackenzie Duntulm 1794 - 1866
Their son
Roderick MacDonald Obe 1825 - 1909
His wife
Sarah Grant Forres 1840 - 1912
Their son
Malcolm MacDonald Kyles 1869 - 1941
His wife
Catherine Maclennan Finsbay 1889 - 1973

A memorial inscription from Rodel on the Isle of Harris. This is a record of three generations of MacDonalds.

Using written records

Most records that we can use now were written in ink on paper, or, up to about 300 years ago, on dried animal skins called parchment or vellum. Some records were made, like Darius's inscription and the Pillar of Eliseg, solely to proclaim lines of ancestry. Most, however, were made for other reasons, to register births, marriages and deaths or to record land ownership. If John died and his son Eric inherited his land, a record of this inheritance of land might record 'Eric son of John'.

Post Card

For Correspondence   Address Only

SCOTTISH BABIES CONTEST

Section ...1...   "SUNDAY MAIL" 1/3/36.

Name (of Parent) (Mrs.) E. H. Fenton

Address   34 Craigpark Drive,
   Glasgow. E.1.

Name of Baby   Alasdair Iain

Age of Baby ...1 Year 10 Months...

How genealogists use records

Our job as family tree explorers is to find records that provide useful information on how people are related to each other. To do so was the idea of a few clever men like the royal herald Sir William Dugdale (1605-1686). He knew that the Tower of London was just one of many places stuffed full of old records going back to the 1200s, and most included details of family relationships. Genealogists started searching through written records for mentions of the family names they wanted to trace. They started organising the records and indexing them, so you could find the names you wanted. Some records had been eaten by mice, or had rotted away. Those that had survived started to be looked after more carefully.

TIP

Working out ages

Always look out for records giving ages, or parents' names. Baby Alisdair's card above tells us roughly when he was born. He was aged one year and 10 months by 1/3/36, ie, 1 March 1936, so we know he was born about April-May 1934.

Making it up

Up to the 1600s, you either had a family tree like the one King Concenn had inscribed on the Pillar of Eliseg, or you didn't. If you had no family tree, but wanted one, you might pay a genealogist to make one up. Many wealthy English families claimed that they were descended from knights who 'came over' the English Channel with William the Conqueror to fight the Battle of Hastings in 1066. Hardly any of William's knights' names are actually known, so it was easy for families to make up stories like this, and get away with it.

I'm sorry to say that when genealogists started using original records, they did not always tell the truth. The client might want to be descended from a 1066 knight, but the genealogist might discover a turnip-chewing peasant called Will of Grotfield instead. What would the genealogist do? He would claim that Will was actually 'Sir William de Grotteville' who had come over with William the Conqueror. And he would hope nobody found out the truth.

Horace Round

Eventually, somebody did. Horace Round (1854-1928) was like the most frightening schoolteacher you've ever met – you make the slightest mistake, and he spends 20 minutes shouting at you to make you feel completely stupid. Horace Round studied as many family trees as he could, comparing each generation of each tree with original records. Whenever he found a mistake, or a deliberate lie, he told everybody.

Frightening though Horace Round was, he made sure that genealogists stuck to the truth. If you can prove something using written records, or someone's reliable memory, write it down. If you cannot, or are unsure, then be honest and say so. You might be able to prove it later: but until you can do so, do not claim that it is true.

Types of record you may find: Family Bibles

Many Christian families used to record details of themselves in Family Bibles. Here (right) we have a page from a Fairfax Family Bible. It shows John and Penelope Fairfax marrying in 1770, and the births of their children Penelope (1771) and Catherine (1772).

You may find loose lists of family births, marriages and deaths, that may once have been tucked into a Bible. The one above is part of a list of the children of Arthur and Julia Hammond, showing that their daughter Maria married Stanislaus Havers, and had a daughter Angela who married Joseph Adolph. It then lists Angela and Joseph's first three children (they had two more later, after this list was written). That's four generations recorded on one scrap of paper.

TIP

Relationships in records

If a child was baptised, the record might say 'Ellen daughter of Hugo and Margaret'. If a young woman married and her father gave the newly-wed couple a dowry, which was money to set up home, the record might say 'Janet daughter of Richard'.

Memorial cards

These are sometimes printed when people die, as a way of remembering them. Here are both sides of a memorial card for a boy called George Lacey Mason. He died in 1862, aged only 12, at Sedgley Park, a Catholic boys' boarding school in Staffordshire. In those days there were far fewer effective medicines for common illnesses like measles, whooping cough and smallpox, and sadly a lot of children died.

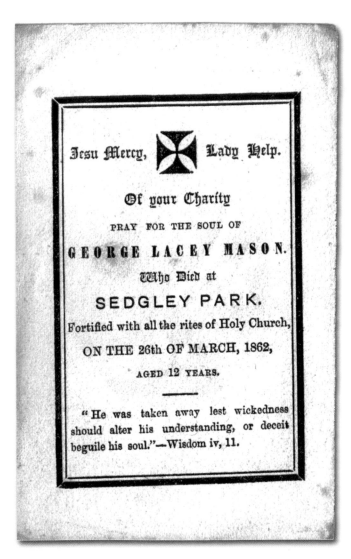

Here are two more memorial cards, for my own great grandparents, who died in the 1960s. They enabled me to add exact dates of death to my family tree.

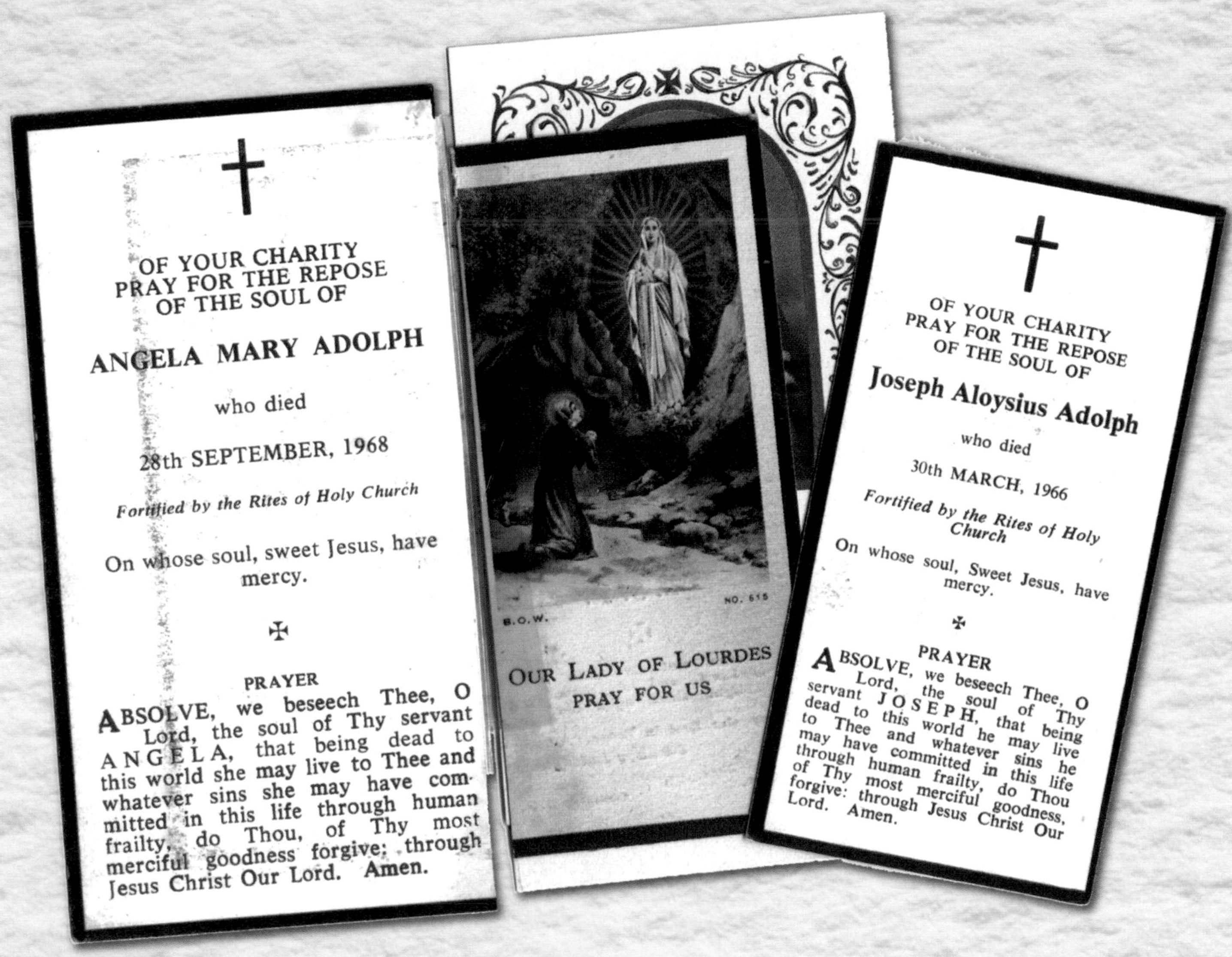

OF YOUR CHARITY
PRAY FOR THE REPOSE
OF THE SOUL OF

ANGELA MARY ADOLPH

who died

28th SEPTEMBER, 1968

Fortified by the Rites of Holy Church

On whose soul, sweet Jesus, have mercy.

✠

PRAYER

ABSOLVE, we beseech Thee, O Lord, the soul of Thy servant ANGELA, that being dead to this world she may live to Thee and whatever sins she may have committed in this life through human frailty, do Thou, of Thy most merciful goodness forgive: through Jesus Christ Our Lord. Amen.

OUR LADY OF LOURDES
PRAY FOR US

NO. 615

B.O.W.

OF YOUR CHARITY
PRAY FOR THE REPOSE
OF THE SOUL OF

Joseph Aloysius Adolph

who died

30th MARCH, 1966

Fortified by the Rites of Holy Church

On whose soul, Sweet Jesus, have mercy.

✠

PRAYER

ABSOLVE, we beseech Thee, O Lord, the soul of Thy servant JOSEPH, that being dead to this world he may live to Thee and whatever sins he may have committed in this life through human frailty, do Thou of Thy most merciful goodness, forgive: through Jesus Christ Our Lord. Amen.

Letters

Before we had e-mails and telephones, people often communicated by letter. To our great grandparents, writing a letter was as normal as sending a text message. Unlike e-mails and text messages, letters were created on pieces of paper, and many were kept. You are likely to come across them in family papers. You can read what your family were doing, 50 or 100 years ago, or even earlier.

My favourite kind of old letters are those written by people who wanted to do what we're doing now – tracing their family trees. Here is a lovely one from my mother's family papers, received by my great grandfather in 1927. It starts:

This is what the original letter looks like. Can you read the old handwriting?

> at East Park Farm,
> Handcross,
> Nr Haywards Heath,
> Sussex
> August 22nd 1927
>
> Dear Sir,
>   You will be surprised to hear from a total stranger.
>   Your mother, Caroline (née Smart) was my second cousin, and I am writing to know if you are able, and will be kind enough to send me any facts about our ancestors prior to:-
>   Benjamin Smart of 60, Princes Street, Leicester Square, London, 1760 – to ---.
> The Christian name of his wife was Lucy.
>   I refer to your Great, Great, Grandfather (my Great Grandfather).

Reading this old letter was the first time I learned that my great grandfather was the great great grandson of Benjamin Smart, so you can just imagine how excited I was when I found it.

Record of Baptisms, Marriages and Burials

Priests and other clergy have special books called Parish Registers, in which they write down when people were buried, married and baptised. The most useful parish records are those of baptisms or christenings (these two words mean the same thing), because these usually record who the child's parents were, taking you back another generation up the family tree. Although some early parish registers date back to 1538, most in England and Wales only survive from the 1600s, in Scotland from the 1700s and Ireland from the 1800s. Christian church records exist all over the world. Most other religions keep similar sorts of records, in synagogues, mosques and temples.

If families wanted a record of a baptism, marriage or burial, they were given a certificate, filled in by the priest. You will sometimes find these in family papers.

Vulnerable records

Many records that were made, recording our ancestors, have been destroyed. Why?
Some have been nibbled by rats
Some have been pecked at by birds
Some have been munched by termites and ants
Some have become damp, and rotted away
Some have been burned in accidental fires
Some have been deliberately thrown out because they were in the way
Some have been stolen
Others have been recycled
So many nasty things can happened to records, it makes you realise how lucky we are that so many have survived!

An old drawing of a church baptism

Parish Registers: Baptisms

This page below is from the parish registers of Great Bookham, Surrey, and was written in 1854. The first entry shows the baptism of John Kemp **(1)** on 22 September 1854, son of James and Sarah Kemp. The family lived in Great Bookham, where James was a labourer, probably on a farm. The next entry **(2)** down shows the baptism on 23 April 1854 of Adeline Baxter. Her parents **(3)** were Samuel and Barbara Baxter of Great Bookham. Samuel was the village police officer. Note the abbreviations used by the vicar: 'and' is written '&' and 'Great' has been shortened to 'Gt'. In the third entry **(4)** the vicar made a mistake over the family's surname, crossed it out and correct it to 'Amey'.

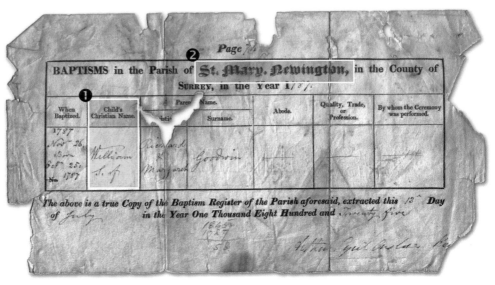

This certificate needs to be handled very carefully in case it falls apart. It shows the baptism of **(1)** William Goodwin, son of Richard and Margaret Goodwin. He was born on 25 October 1787 and baptised at **(2)** St Mary, Newington, Surrey on 26 November the same year. When the original record was made, the 'abode' or home and 'quality, trade or profession' – a rather grand way of saying the job of the father, were not recorded.

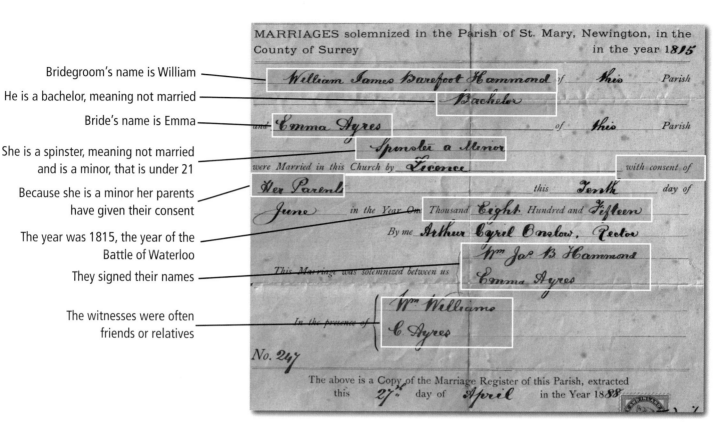

Bridegroom's name is William

He is a bachelor, meaning not married

Bride's name is Emma

She is a spinster, meaning not married and is a minor, that is under 21

Because she is a minor her parents have given their consent

The year was 1815, the year of the Battle of Waterloo

They signed their names

The witnesses were often friends or relatives

Parish Registers: Marriages

This is a marriage certificate from St Mary, Newington, Surrey. It shows the marriage of the rather grandly named William James Barefoot Hammond and Emma Ayres on 10 June 1815 (it took place only eight days before the famous Battle of Waterloo, when the Duke of Wellington defeated Napoleon of France). William was a 'bachelor' and Emma was a 'spinster', meaning that neither of them had been married before. Both were 'of this parish', so lived in St Mary, Newington. Emma was 'a minor', a term used for anyone under the age of 21, and it adds that she married 'with consent of her parents': if her parents had said 'no', she could not have married. At the very bottom it says that the certificate was filled in on 27 April 1888, presumably having been requested by one of their children or grandchildren, perhaps someone trying to explore the family tree themselves.

Parish Registers: Burials

A page from the **(1)** burial register of St John's, Hackney, London. The first entry shows that **(2)** John Thomas Rudrum who lived at 38, The Grove, Hackney, had been buried on **(3)** 22 December 1891, **(4)** aged 85. He would therefore have been born about 1806.

Name.	Abode.	When buried.	Age.	By whom the Ceremony was performed.
John Thomas Rudrum No. 1457	38 The Grove	December 22	85	Cyril Stanley Curate
George Frederick Taylor No. 1458	126 Wells Street	1892 January 14th	77	Edwin Noyes Curate
Sarah Goodwin No. 1459	90 Median Rd.	1892 January 27th	80	G. H. Newton Curate
Emma Martha Aubert No. 1460	1 Lee Place Clapton	1892 February 17.	82	D. Shepard Rector of Stoke Newington
Mary Willis No. 1461	62 North Street	1892 March 19	73	John C. Mann Curate of Christ Church S.H
Emma Maria Carruthers No. 1462	Cambridge Rd Bethnal Green	1892 March 23	78	G. H. Newton Curate.
Elizabeth Allen No. 1463	38 Marmora Road Honor Oak	1892 April 20	81	G. H. Newton Curate.
Rebecca Goodwin No. 1464	121 Almack Road	May 20th 1892	79	Edwin Noyes Curate

BURIALS in the Parish of *Hackney* **①** in the County of *London* in the year One thousand eight hundred and *ninety one & Ninety Two*

Wills

People sometimes write wills to say what they want to happen to their property after they have gone. Family wills are interesting because they might tell you what property ancestors had – sometimes people describe their homes, books, clothes and furniture and occasionally mention old family portraits. Mainly, wills are useful because people name their relatives. Someone writing a will might say 'to my son Arthur I leave my stuffed parrot', and from this you learn who Arthur's father was (and where that stuffed parrot came from). They may mention brothers and sisters, nieces and nephews and even cousins. A detailed will can give you all sorts of new details for the family tree.

This is a will from 1929. The language is fairly complicated, because it is written by lawyers, but the details for the family tree are simple enough. Mary Denning had a son, William Patrick Denning, and a daughter, Mary Josephine Denning. Because she was still using the name Denning, we can tell that Mary Josephine was not married by 1929.

her daughter is called Mary

Date of the will

Mary Denning's will

Mary Denning's address

THIS IS THE LAST WILL AND TESTAMENT of me MARY DENNING of "Knocka-tane" South Drive Ruislip in the County of Middlesex made this 21st August 1929 day of _ in the year of our Lord one thousand nine hundred and twenty nine I hereby revoke all wills made by me at any time heretofore I appoint my son William Patrick Paul Denning to be my EXECUTOR and direct that all my debts and funeral expenses shall be paid as soon as conveniently may be after my decease I give and bequeath unto my daughter Mary Josephine Denning my house known as "Knockatane" situate in South Drive Ruislip together with all the contents thereof my said son William Patrick Paul Denning all shares & moneys standing in my name to be used in accordance with my wishes as expressed to him - MARY DENNING - Signed by the said testator Mary Denning in the presence of us present at the same time who at her request in her presence and in the presence of each other have subscribed our names as witnesses MAY A HOWARD Stanbridge North Drive Ruislip - MARJORY K HOWARD Stanbridge North Drive Ruislip -

Proved 22nd October 1929.

The date of the will 'proved' or 'registered' after Mary has died

her son is called William

CERTIFIED COPY OF AN ENTRY OF BIRTH

GIVEN AT THE G

Application Number

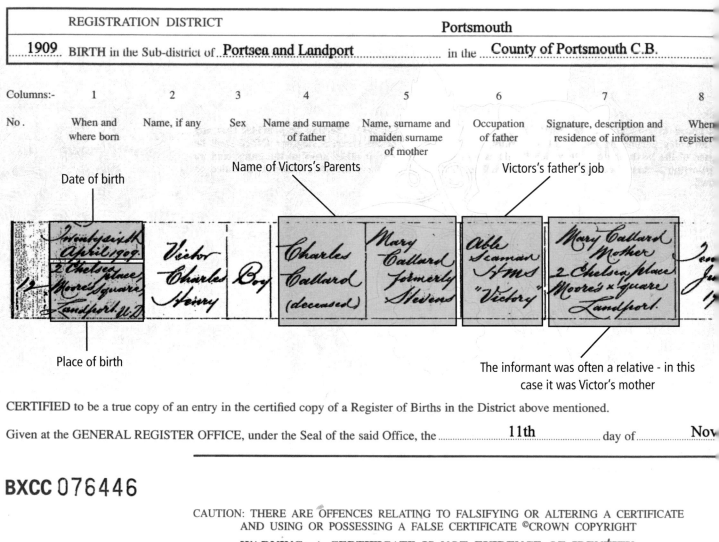

		REGISTRATION DISTRICT			Portsmouth		

1909 BIRTH in the Sub-district of **Portsea and Landport** in the **County of Portsmouth C.B.**

Columns:- 1 2 3 4 5 6 7 8

No.	When and where born	Name, if any	Sex	Name and surname of father	Name, surname and maiden surname of mother	Occupation of father	Signature, description and residence of informant	When register

Date of birth

Name of Victors's Parents

Victors's father's job

| Twenty sixth April 1909. 2 Chelsea Place, Moores Square, Landport U.D. | Victor Charles Henry | Boy | Charles Callard (deceased) | Mary Callard formerly Stevens | Able Seaman HMS "Victory" | Mary Callard Mother 2 Chelsea Place Moore's square Landport. |

Place of birth

The informant was often a relative - in this case it was Victor's mother

CERTIFIED to be a true copy of an entry in the certified copy of a Register of Births in the District above mentioned.

Given at the GENERAL REGISTER OFFICE, under the Seal of the said Office, the .... **11th** .... day of .... Nov

BXCC 076446

039887 10107 08/05 SPSL 012033

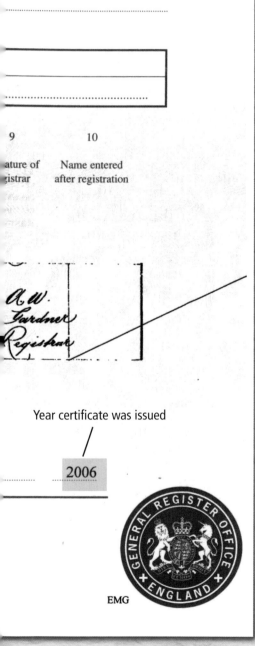

L REGISTER OFFICE

9   10

ature of   Name entered
gistrar   after registration

A.W.
Gardner
Registrar

Year certificate was issued

2006

GENERAL REGISTER OFFICE ENGLAND

EMG

Types of records you might find: Birth certificates

When you are born, marry or die, government officials called Registrars make a record. These records are called Birth, Marriage and Death Certificates. These have been made in England and Wales since 1837, in Scotland since 1855 and in Ireland since 1864. Similar records are kept in many other countries.

Birth certificates are the most useful of all, because they usually say who both the child's parents were. Depending on which country you are in, parents' names may appear on marriage and death records too. Ask your parents if they have a copy of your birth certificate, so you can see what information appears on it.

This birth certificate shows the birth of Victor Charles Henry Callard. Victor was born on 26 April 1909 at 2 Chelsea Place, Moore's Square, Landport, which is part of the great Royal Navy base at Portsmouth, Hampshire. Victor's mother was Mary Callard formerly Stevens – Stevens was her maiden name, the name she had before she was married. Victor's father was Charles Callard, an able seaman on H.M.S. *Victory*. An Able Seaman was an ordinary sailor. His Majesty's Ship *Victory* is one of the most famous British warships. Back in 1805, it was the ship in which the great Admiral Lord Nelson defeated the French at the Battle of Trafalgar. The certificate shows an interesting detail – Victor's father Charles was 'deceased'. This means he had died, presumably while his wife Maria was pregnant. Poor Victor would never have known his father.

Types of records you might find: Marriage certificates

This is the marriage certificate of Victor's parents, Charles Callard and Mary Stevens. They married on 4 June 1900 at St Agatha's Church, Portsea, next to Portsmouth. Charles was an Able Seaman, then serving on H.M.S. *Resolution*, and Mary had been working as a domestic servant, a maid in someone's home. The certificate says how old they were – Charles was 21, and Mary was 19. It names both their fathers. Charles's father Charles Callard was a labourer. Mary's was more exciting – Guiseppe di Stefano, a harpist. I discovered that Guiseppe had come from Sicily. 'Di Stefano' is the Italian for Stevens (both names mean 'child of Stephen'), so it looks as if Mary had started using the English version of the name, perhaps because she did not want people to think she was foreign.

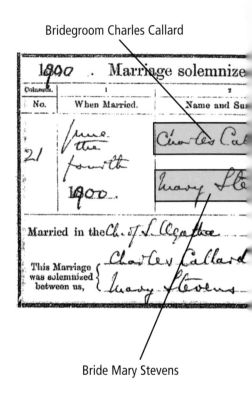

Bridegroom Charles Callard

Bride Mary Stevens

OF MARRIAGE   GIVEN AT THE GENERAL REGISTER OFFICE

W132096

Application Number ....

Charles Callard's occupation

Charles's father's name and job

	Church of S. Agatha in the *Parish* of *Portsea*			in the County *of Northampton*		
Age.	Condition.	Rank or Profession.	Residence at the time of Marriage.	Father's Name and Surname.	Rank or Profession of Father.
21	Bachelor	Able Seaman R.N.	H.M.S. "Revolution"	Charles Callard	Labourer
19	Spinster	Domestic Servant	15 Staunton St.	Guiseppe di Stefano (Stevens)	Harpist.

to the Rites and Ceremonies of the Church of England ~~by~~ *or after* banns *by me,*

George Herbert Trevenhen

    in the Presence of us   }   Luigi + de'Luchi, his mark

Emma di Stefano.

Mary Stevens' occupation

It looks as if both witness were Italian, like Mary herself

...rtified copy of a register of Marriages in the Registration District of   **Portsmouth** ....

Seal of the said Office, the   **20th**   *day of*   **November**   **2006**

CERTIFIED COPY OF AN ENTRY OF DEATH

GIVEN

Applicat

REGISTRATION DISTRICT		Lewisham		
1915 DEATH in the Sub-district of Lee		in the County of London		

Columns:– 1 2 3 4 5 6 7

No.	When and where died	Name and surname	Sex	Age	Occupation	Cause of death	Signature, description and residence of informant
				Arthur's age			
49	Fourteenth October 1915 8 Dorville Road	Arthur Stanley	Male	63 Years	Retired Silk Mercer	Incompetence of Aortic valves of the Heart and fracture of the 1st Cervical Vertebra due to fall into an Area while watching the effects of Gun fire during Zeppelin Airship raid. Accidental Causes. P.m.	Certificate received from H. R. Oswald Coroner for County of Inquest held Eighteenth Octobe 1915

Arthur's Stanley is the dead person's name

Arthur's Stanley's occupation

The cause of Arthur's Stanley's death

CERTIFIED to be a true copy of an entry in the certified copy of a Register of Deaths in the District above mentioned.

Given at the GENERAL REGISTER OFFICE, under the Seal of the said Office, the .... 23rd .... day of ....

DYA 751605

CAUTION: THERE ARE OFFENCES RELATING TO FALSIFYING OR ALTERING A CERTIFICATE AND USING OR POSSESSING A FALSE CERTIFICATE ©CROWN COPYRIGHT
WARNING: A CERTIFICATE IS NOT EVIDENCE OF IDENTITY.

036563 9199 04/05 SPSL 010695

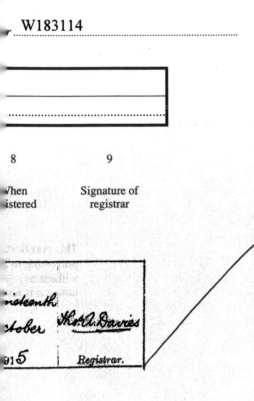

GENERAL REGISTER OFFICE

W183114

8	9
When istered	Signature of registrar

ineteenth
tober
915 | *Thos. A. Davies*
Registrar.

2005

See note overleaf

GCJ

Types of records you might find: Death certificates

This is the death certificate of Arthur Stanley, who died on 14 October 1915 at 8 Darville Road, Lewisham, London. It says that he was 63 years old, and was a retired silk mercer (someone who sold silk).

The 'cause of death' sometimes tells a story. He died of 'incompetence of aortic valves of the Heart and fracture of the 1st cervical vertebra due to fall into an Area while watching the effects of Gun Fire during Zeppelin Airship raid'.

This death took place half way through the First World War (1914-18). Put simply, Arthur was standing on a wall in his garden, watching a German airship trying to bomb London, and he fell off, broke his back and had a heart attack.

Types of records you might find: Censuses

Every ten years, from 1841 onwards, the government has taken a census. On the appointed evening, census recorders, called 'enumerators', went from door to door. They would ask who was staying there that night, and write down the answers on forms, one per household. The 1841 census was not very detailed – they asked for names, jobs, rough ages

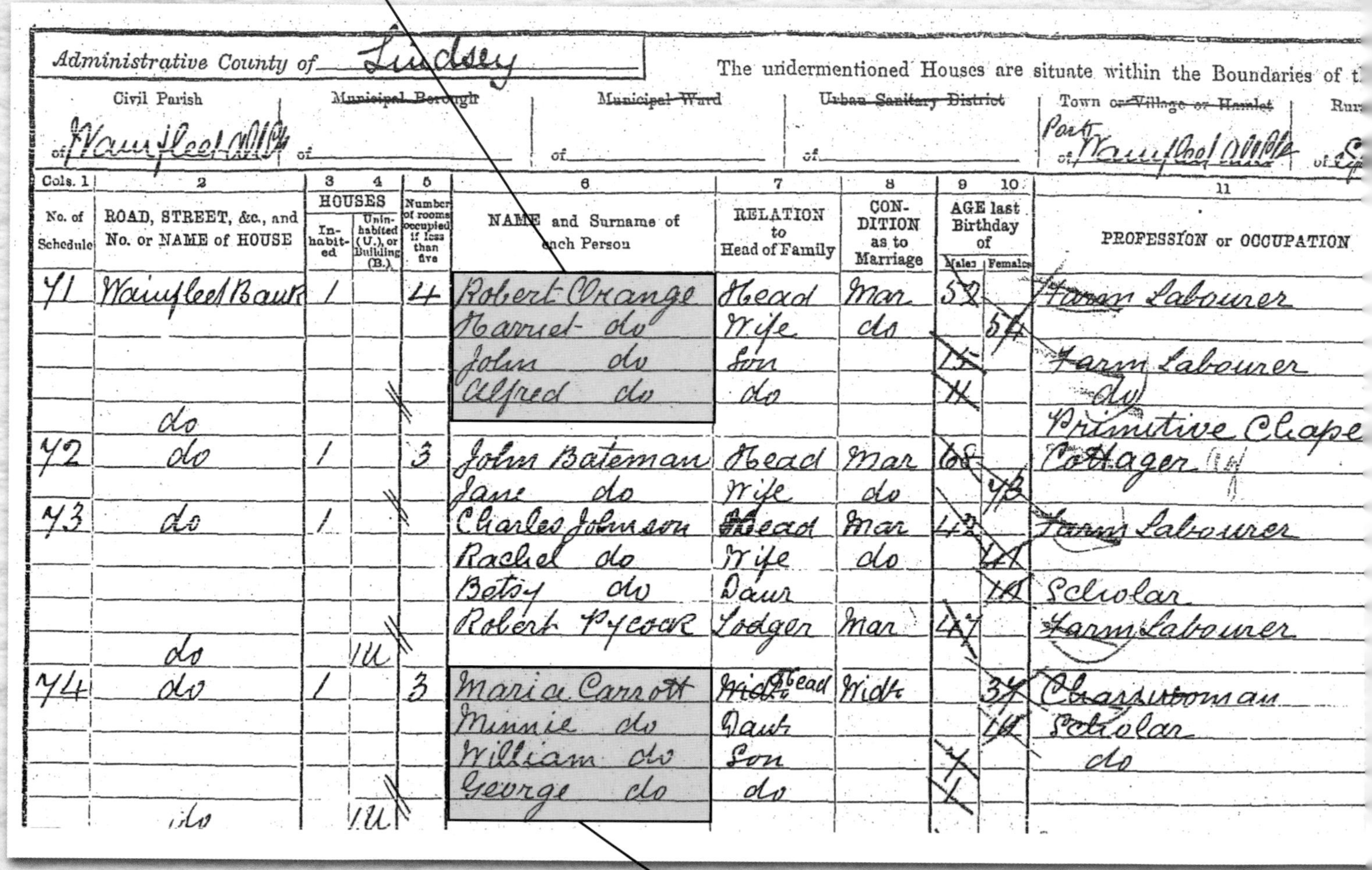

Orange family

Part of the 1891 census for Wainfleet

Carrott family

and whether people had been born in the county in which they now lived. From 1851, they asked for names, exact ages, how everyone present was related to the head of the family, jobs, how old they were and where they had been born.

The censuses for approximately the last 100 years exist, but are kept secret. The earlier ones can be seen by anyone. Looking at a census is like peering down from the clouds at your family in the past.

The picture here is an amusing but true entry from the 1891 census of the parish of Wainfleet All Saints, Lincolnshire. The first household listed is headed by Robert Orange, aged 52. With him was his wife Harriet Orange, and their children John Orange, 15 and Alfred Orange, 11. Three doors away down the lane, after the Bateman and Johnson families, was the Carrott family. Maria Carrott is listed first: she was a widow (her husband had died) aged 37. With her were three children, Minnie Carrott, 10, William Carrott, 7 and George Carrott, 1.

The word 'do' is short for 'ditto', meaning that the word written directly above is repeated. Thus, 'Harriet do' written straight below Robert Orange means her name was Harriet Orange.

You can work out roughly when they were all born by subtracting the ages from the census year, 1891. For example, Harriet Orange was 54 in 1891, so 1891 – 54 = 1837. The last column tells you where everyone was born – the Oranges and Carrots were born in different parishes in Lincolnshire. Minnie Carrott, for example, would have been born about 1881 in Wainfleet.

The column headed 'profession or occupation' hints at what life was like for these two families. Robert Orange and his sons were all farm labourers, even though the boys were only 15 and 11. Mrs Carrott's two elder children, Minnie and William, were 'scholars'. This sounds rather grand, but it means simply that they were at school.

Combining different records:

Document One

Genealogists work back from what we know for sure, to find out new things. Often, you find the truth by combining different records together. In my case, my great grandfather Joseph Adolph's marriage certificate showed that he had been born in about 1881-2, son of Albert Adolph. That means that when the 1901 census was taken he should have been aged about 18 or19. His family, in fact, appears as follows:

Great grandfather Joseph Adolph is recorded in this census. He is 18 years old

No of Schedule	ROAD, STREET, &c., and No. or NAME of HOUSE	Inhabited	In Occupation.	Not in Occupation.	Building.	Number of Rooms occupied if less than five	Name and Surname of each Person	RELATION to Head of Family	Condition as to Marriage	Age
148	Corsica	1					Albert J. Adolph	Head	M	46
	Montefiore Rd.						Emily A. D	Wife	M	
							Joseph D	Son	S	18
							William D	Son	S	15
							Grace D	Daur	S	
							Maud D	Daur.	S	
							Cecil D	Son	S	8
							Monica D	Daur.	S	
							Emma Mowles	Servant	S	
							Alice E. Gales	Servant	S	
149	Patea	1					Richard T. Southby	Head	S	53

1901 census

'Corsica' is the name of the house in Montefiore Road, Hove, where the family lived.

Joseph Adolph was born in London

re situate within the boundaries of the

cipal Borough n District	Rural District		Parliamentary Borough or Division	Town or V
Ward parh of	of		of _Brighton Part_	of

13	14	15	16	
PROFESSION OR OCCUPATION	Employer, Worker, or Own account	If Working at Home	WHERE BORN	(1) (2) (3) (4)
dolph Merchant of General Merchandise	Employer		London	✓
			London	✓
			London	✓
			London	✓
			London	✓
			Sussex Brighton	
			Sussex Brighton	
			Sussex Brighton	
Cook (Domestic)			Suffolk Chatfield	✓
Housemaid (Domestic)			Sussex Hove	
Parlourmaid (Domestic)			Berks East Ileen	✓

Joseph's father was an 'export merchant of general merchadise'

Combining different records

Document Two

The census tells me all about his family at the time, but most importantly that he and his parents (Albert, 46 and Emily, 44) were all born in London.

  If Albert was 46 in 1901, then he was probably aged about 16 in the 1871 census. Here he is:

1871 Census

No. of Schedule	ROAD, STREET, &c., and No. or NAME of HOUSE	HOUSES Inhabit-ed	HOUSES Unin-habited (U.), or Building (B.)	NAME and Surname of each Person	RELATION to Head of Family	CON-DITION	AGE of Males	AGE of Females
233	22 "	1		Albert Adolph	Head	M	55	
				Jane "	neice			28
				Alpheus "	nephew		20	
				Albert "	"		16	
				Hannah Sahee	Serv			36

Here is Albert Adolph at 16 and working as an apprentice

  This was a stroke of luck, because I knew the family was from Germany, but did not know where. Here, 16-year-old Albert is listed with his uncle, Albert, 55, born in 'Hachenburg, Nassau, Naturalised British Sub[ject]'. Nassau is in modern Germany, and so here was proof of where my family originated. To be absolutely sure the entries fitted together,

I also obtained Joseph's birth certificate, and the marriage and birth records of his father Albert, to confirm the line beyond doubt and make sure I had not made a mistaken identification.

Going back to the early 1800s takes you back before censuses and General Registration. So, at this point you can start using parish registers to explore your family line back into the 1700s and, with any luck, beyond.

The place of birth of Albert junior's Uncle Albert: Hachenburg, Nassau

Decoding old handwriting

You will find some records that you just cannot read because the handwriting is old fashioned, or unclear. I know this because, in my work, I often sit staring at old records, working out what they say. Sometimes, it is worth just asking other people around if they can read something you cannot. You can also try to decode old handwriting yourself. Look for words that you can read, and see how each individual letter has been written. In a word you cannot read, see if any of those letters appear. Say (just for example) that you are unsure about William Bassett's middle name, because of that rather odd ∧ shape in it. On the left, is the date, '4th January 1907'. You know that the 6th letter of January is an 'r', and here it is written with the same ∧ shape. This is in fact one way in which 'r's used to be written. So that letter in the name (which of course says 'Henry') is an 'r'.

Create your own census returns

The censuses we use for genealogy today were made by 'enumerators' filling in details of each household, house by house, street by street. They are wonderful historical records. You can make a few of your own that future generations of your family will appreciate.

1 Photocopy or copy the form below by hand. This form has ten rows: if you need more, add them on below using a pencil and ruler.

2 Fill in details for everyone who will be staying in your home tonight. Start with the head of the household. This will be the person who pays the bills. Write their full name including middle names and surname.

3 List everybody else below, and in the 'relationship' column fill in how they are related to the 'head'. The 'relationship' might be 'husband', 'wife', 'son', 'daughter', or 'guest', 'lodger', grandmother', and so on. 'Condition' means whether you are married or unmarried. If someone was born outside Great Britain, write the country of birth in the 'county' column.

TIP Don't assume you know things about other people when you are not absolutely sure: your job as a good census enumerator is to ask each person for their accurate details.

CENSUS FORM

Full address _____

_____

Date (day, month , year)

FULL NAME	RELATION TO HEAD OF HOUSEHOLD

Don't just do this once. Whenever you have relatives staying, take another census. Keep them all together. As with photographs, the details you record may seem incredibly obvious to you now. But in the future people will be just as fascinated by what you have recorded as you are by what was written down in old records that exist now.

This form was enumerated by: _____

mar=married; umn=unmarried; dau=daughter; do=ditto

CONDITION (married/ unmarried)	AGE	RANK/OCCUPATION	COUNTY OF BIRTH	PLACE OF BIRTH

Chapter 14

Where Next? Visiting archives and ancestral homes

Eventually, you will have found out so much from your relatives, that they just won't be able to tell you any more. But you can find out more yourself. You can explore places where your family lived, and perhaps visit an archive to look for new records to do with your ancestors.

Exploring ancestral homes

Ask your parents if you may visit places where your family used to live. Your parents or grandparents may enjoy a 'trip down memory lane' by taking you to explore where they used to live. Or they may enjoy visiting places for the first time, where their own parents or grandparents lived. If this is not possible to do now, remember the names of your 'ancestral homes'. You never know when you may be passing by in the future.

When you go exploring, try to take a camera and a notebook, to record your experiences.

If you know the exact addresses where people in your family lived, try to find these now. Some old homes were bombed in the Second World War, or have just been demolished to make way for newer homes, roads, railways or supermarkets. I once discovered that my mother's great great grandparents had lived in a big house quite near me in Stoke Newington, London. I worked out exactly where it was, and went to the site. I discovered that their home had been demolished to make way for the car park of the new council offices. I was rather disappointed, but at least I now have a photograph of me standing in a car park where my great, great, great grandparents used to live in their house.

Me in the council office car park, on the site of the house where my family used to live, 150 years ago.

Things to look out for

Look out for old post boxes, buildings or even trees that may have been there when your ancestors were alive. In the example above, my ancestor's house is no longer there, but the old parish church next door is. The view I saw from the car park was probably much the same as my ancestors saw when they lived there.

Growing my family tree

When I began to grow my family tree,
It was a little seedling showing me,
And mummy, daddy, and my brother Joe:
I watered it and hoped that it would grow.

My uncles and my aunts I added on,
And all their children, even cousin Ron,
Who won a second prize for ten-pin bowling,
And cousin Fred, who once met J.K. Rowling.

My family tree had started now to grow,
But still looked rather straggly and so,
I telephoned my grandparents to ask
If they could help me carry on my task.

They told me all the names and dates they knew
About their sisters and their brothers too,
Including my great uncle George who once
Got married in a railway train in France.

The family tree was looking taller now,
With names and dates like leaves on every bough:
And granny gave me lots of details for
Great grandpa, who was in the First World War.

Just when I thought my tree had stopped to rise,
I had a simply marvellous surprise:
An e-mail from my aunt in Lowestoft –
She'd found some family papers in the loft!

These gave me loads of extra names and dates,
And marriage, birth and death certificates,
And funeral cards inscribed with 'In Memoria'
That went back to the time of Queen Victoria.

My family tree is now so tall that I,
Can climb right up and almost reach the sky.
But it's such fun, I'm very glad to know –
My tree has got a great deal more to grow!

A.A.

Have a look in the local graveyard and see if you can spot any gravestones with your family names on them.

Use a notebook to copy down exactly what is written on the gravestones. You may not know how these people fit into your family tree at the time, but you may be able to find out later.

See if there are any postcards for sale in local shops showing the place as it is now. Sometimes you can buy postcards with old pictures of the place too, showing what it was like when your ancestors lived there.

Scott Crowley recording the wording on his great grandfather's gravestone, during a trip to Lochinver, Scotland.

Local museums and archives

See if there is a local museum you can explore. It is worth finding out about museums and local archives on the Internet before you leave home, especially to check when they will be open. Here are some lists of links to archives and museums:

England and Wales **www.a2a.org.uk/search/index.asp** under 'location of archives'
Scotland **www.scan.org.uk/** under 'directory'
Ireland's Heritage Centres are listed at **www.irish-roots.net** under 'county centres'

Museums may tell you much about life in your 'ancestral home' in the past, providing details on local foods, songs or clothes. Tell the staff why you are there, as you never know – they might have heard of your family.

Local archives and local studies libraries (which are often attached to ordinary libraries) often have old books about the area. They may also have collections of old photographs that will show you what it was like too.

Further reading

I have written several books explaining how to undertake original research in archives and using the records now available on the Internet:

Anthony Adolph, *Need to Know? Tracing Your Family History* (Collins, 2007) is simple guide to British research starting with the absolute basics.

Anthony Adolph, *Tracing Your Family History* (Collins, 2005) is a much more detailed guide to research, though also starting right from the beginning. It also shows how to use records similar to those found in Britain in other countries, and has a special focus on the Caribbean.

Anthony Adolph, *Tracing Your Irish Family History* (Collins, 2007) is for anyone with Irish roots, and starts by explaining how to explore back to Ireland from abroad.

Anthony Adolph, *Tracing Your Scottish Family History* (Collins, 2008) does the same job for people with Scottish roots, also starting with how to trace back to Scotland from abroad.

For dating old photograph, see Jayne Shrimptons' *Family Photographs and How to Date Them* (Countryside Books, 2008)

I also recommend:
Sir Anthony Wagner's *Pedigree and Progress* (Phillimore, 1975) and Sir Iain Moncreiffe's *Royal Highness: Ancestry of the Royal Child* (Hamish Hamilton, 1982) contain the most fascinating family trees, connecting royalty all around the world, and many more normal families as well.

Chris Pomery's *Family History in the Genes* (National Archives, 2007), explaining more about DNA and how to use it for family tree research.

www.everygeneration.co.uk Patrick Vernon's website, aimed at encouraging black children to explore and take pride in their roots.

Some very good surname dictionaries are:
P.H. Reaney and R.M. Wilson's *A Dictionary of English Surnames,* (Oxford University Press, 2005)
J. Rowlands's *Welsh Family History; a guide to research* (Association of Family History Societies for Wales, 1997)
G.F. Black's *The Surnames of Scotland, Their Origin, Meaning, and History* (New York Public Library, 1946)
E. MacLysaght's *The Surnames of Ireland* (Irish Academic Press, 1985)

www.genesreunited.co.uk You can enter your family tree onto this site. If anyone else on the site has the same name or names in their family tree, you will be told. For a small membership fee, you will then be able to contact them to find out if you are related.

In good newsagents such as W.H. Smith's you will find a number of excellent genealogy magazines: *Family History Monthly; Your Family Tree; Practical Family History; Family Tree Magazine, Ancestors* and *Why Do You Think You Are? Magazine.*

ACTIVITY

Grow a family "tree"

1 Ask your grandparents for some seeds or a cutting from a plant in their garden (or in their house).

2 Plant the seeds, or put the cutting in water, until it produces roots, and then plant it in the garden or a window box.

3 Make a plaque out of a piece of stone or pottery to say why this plant is special. Acrylic paint is best for outdoor painting. You can varnish the plaque to make sure it lasts.

4 Water your plant, look after it and enjoy it growing.

You will now have a plant that comes from one owned by your grandparents – just as you, in your own way, come from your grandparents too.

TIP

If your grandparents have died, you could take some seeds or a cutting from a plant growing where they are buried, or where their ashes were scattered, or even just from a place that you know was special to them.

If the plant you choose is a tree, then you really can say it is a family tree!

A final word of encouragement

I hope you have enjoyed exploring your family tree. I made my first family tree in 1978, when I was 10, and I am still drawing them now. I couldn't have found a more interesting pastime. I have met distant relatives from all over the world, and have visited some of them in their own countries. I have found distant connections to artists, writers, warriors and ancient kings. Through my family tree, I have learned all about our human history, and even studied our earlier family tree, going back to the very origins of life. I have been lucky enough to make it my career as well. Maybe some of you will do the same.

The world's archives and libraries are full of records that can be used to find out more about your own ancestors. However far your explorations have taken you, I guarantee that you will always have more to find. The wonderful thing about genealogy and family history is that you have never finished. There is always something else out there, just waiting out to be discovered.

Index

Figures in *italics* indicate captions to illustrations.

PICTURE CREDITS
The publishers would like to thank and acknowledge the following for images reproduced in this book:
KEY: a above, b below, c centre, l left, r right

7 John Cowie/Shutterstock; 9 Online Creative Media/iStockphoto; 13 Propix inc/iStockphoto; 14 Mary Evans Picture Library/Alamy; 17 Photo12.com – ARJ; 18l Holmes Garden Photos/Alamy; 18r Edd Westmacott/Alamy; 19l Giangrande Alessia/Shutterstock; 19r Ruta Saulyte-Laurinaviciene/Shutterstock; 32 Sandro Vannini/Corbis; 41 Getty Images; 42 Julie Keen/Shutterstock; 46a Rex Features; 58l Bettmann/Corbis; 58r Roussel/Apis/Sygma/Corbis; 61, 62 Photo12.com - Collection Cinéma; 67 Getty Images; 68b Gail Mooney/Corbis; 69 Bob Krist/Corbis; 73a Monkey Business Images/Shutterstock; 75 Ian Goodrick/Alamy; 77 Chris Homfray; 79 Martin Novak/Shutterstock; 83 Fletcher/Rex Features; 85a www.white-windmill.co.uk/Alamy; 86l The Print Collector/Alamy; 89 Peter Schouten/National Geographic Society/Reuters/Corbis; 90l Pixelman/Shutterstock; 91 Bestweb/Shutterstock; 93 Jurgen Ziewe/Shutterstock; 94 English School/Getty Images; 95 Fine Art Photographic Library/Corbis; 96 Antiques & Collectables/Alamy; 97a Interfoto Pressebildagentur/Alamy; 97b Dorling Kindersley/Getty Images; 98 Bettmann/Corbis; 99a E.O. Hoppé/Corbis; 99b Yasonya/Shutterstock; 100a Dmitri Baltermants/The Dmitri Baltermants Collection/Corbis; 101a, 100b Bettmann/Corbis; 101b TopFoto; 102 Time & Life Pictures/Getty Images; 103, 106 Getty Images; 107a School of Sir Peter Lely/Getty Images; 107b The Print Collector/Alamy; 109 Christopher Poe/Shutterstock; 111al Kelvin Wakefield/iStockphoto; 111ar Carlos E. Santa Maria/Shutterstock; 111bl Carme Balcells/Shutterstock; 111br Johnnychaos/Shutterstock; 112 Alexander Ishchenko/Shutterstock; 114a Frame in Time Photography/iStockphoto; 114b Steve Taylor/Alamy; 115 Christopher Wood Gallery, London, UK/The Bridgeman Art Library; 116 Central Press/Getty Images; 117 Manchester Art Gallery, UK/The Bridgeman Art Library; 120 H. Armstrong Roberts/ClassicStock/TopFoto; 121 Ariel Skelley/Corbis; 124 Nikolay Okhitin/Shutterstock; 125a Ashmolean Museum, University of Oxford, UK/The Bridgeman Art Library; 125b Syamsul Bahri Muhammad/Shutterstock; 126a, 127b Bettmann/Corbis; 128 Leslie Garland Picture Library/Alamy; 134 Mike Harrington/Alamy; 138 Sergey Lavrentev/Shutterstock; 140 Vasiliy Koval/Shutterstock; 141 Nicolas McComber/Shutterstock; 143 Elena Kalistratova/Shutterstock; 144 Dhoxax/Shutterstock; 145 Francis G. Mayer/Corbis; 147a Underwood & Underwood/Corbis; 147b Richard Griffin/Shutterstock; 148 English School/Getty Images; 149 PatternKing/Shutterstock; 152b Liette Parent/Shutterstock; 153a Elena Blokhina/Shutterstock; 153c Brian Weed/Shutterstock; 153b ArrowStudio, LLC/Shutterstock; 158a Richard Griffin/Shutterstock; 158c Ken Schulze/Shutterstock; 158b Fernando Blanco Calzada/Shutterstock; 158r Elena Elisseeva/Shutterstock; 160l Ashley Whitworth/Shutterstock; 160c Alice/Shutterstock; 160r Torsten Lorenz/Shutterstock; 161 Lukáš Hejtman/Shutterstock; 163b Getty Images; 164 Alexander Motrenko/Shutterstock; 169 Chris Howes/Wild Places Photography/Alamy; 172 The National Archives; 177r Nattika/Shutterstock; 178-193 © Crown copyright material is reproduced with the permission of the Controller of HMSO and Queen's Printer for Scotland; 200 Elnur Motrenko/Shutterstock; 202 Plusphoto/Shutterstock

THE AUTHOR'S ACKNOWLEDGEMENTS
My mother, Mrs Jane Adolph; Alexandra Barkshire; Nancy Bedwell; Dean Bubier; Steve Butters (Maine Coon Cat Club); Phoebe and Ji Sun Capon; Baz Crowe; Mr and Mrs Tony Crow; Andrew Crowley; Scott Crowley; Kay Cullen (MacLeod Family Collection); Eleanor English; Elizabeth English; Frederick English; Madeleine English; Adam Green; Emma and Paul Head; Suzy Jenvey; Michael Kan; Tom Meek; Mrs Louise Norman; Mewey Pooey; Anna Power; Sarah Warwick (Family History Monthly); Miriam Watson; Ken Miller and Valerie Weeks.

FURTHER THANKS
Thanks to the Tolkien Estate for their kind permission to reproduce the quotation on page 2 and the Baggins' family tree on page 64, both which are derived from *The Lord of the Rings* ©The J.R.R. Tolkien Copyright Trust 1937, 1951, 1966, 1978, 1995; Thanks to HarperCollins Publishers Ltd for the permission to reprint this material. The image of Perry Nursey on page 51 has been reproduced courtesy of Suffolk Record Office, Ipswich Branch, ref HD480/2.